HORSEMAN'S HANDBOOK

HORSE OWNERSHIP, CARE & ENJOYMENT

by Joe B. Armstrong

Published 2023 in New Mexico by Gunsight Media.
Library of Congress Control Number: 2023913557
ISBN 9798988710905

Written by Joe H.B. Armstrong Sr., Ph.D.
With contribution by J.H.B. Armstrong, Jr.
Illustrated & formatted by Edward R. Armstrong

Publisher's Cataloging-in-Publication Data
Names: Armstrong, Joe B., 1937– author.
Title: Horseman's handbook : horse ownership, care and enjoyment / Joe B. Armstrong cattleman, horseman and PhD.
Description: La Mesa, New Mexico : Gunsight Media, 2023. | Includes bibliographical references and index.
Identifiers: LCCN 2023913557 | ISBN 9798988710905 (pbk.) | ISBN 9798988710912 (ebook)
Subjects: LCSH: Horses – Care. | Horses – Health. | Horses – Riding. | Horses – Training. | Horse owners.
Classification: LCC SF285 2023 | DDC 636.1

Printed in the United States of America on paper sourced from Forest Stewardship Council® certified forests.
26 25 24 23 5 4 3 2 1

HORSEMAN'S HANDBOOK

GUNSIGHT MEDIA
PUBLISHED IN LA MESA, NEW MEXICO
PRINTED IN UNITED STATES OF AMERICA

Armstrong Equine Service
https://armstrongequine.com

WARNING

ALL activities involving HORSES, donkeys, mules or ponies have inherent risks for participants.

New Mexico State law protects operators, owners, trainers, promoters and others from liability for injuries which are the result of an equine animal's behavior.

USE THESE FACILITIES AND/OR RIDE AT YOUR OWN RISK

Equine Liability Act SJC/Senate Bill 268.aa1993

FOREWORD

by B.F. Yeates

WOW! What a book that my friend and former co-worker Joe Armstrong has put together. This book captures a lifetime of knowledge and experience with horses, both professional and private. Joe has lived what he is writing about. He has addressed the knowledge and skills that horse owners need with great illustrations to provide a better understanding.

In my lifetime, I've observed many great horsemen practicing their profession in a lot of different ways. Many have been successful. There are few who will take the time to share with others, and even fewer who can share in a way that can be easily understood. Joe is one of these rare individuals.

This is a book about horses – one of God's great Creations for man to use in all his endeavors – and I feel compelled to point out that the Bible mentions horses 188 times. America was built with horsepower before mechanization became a reality. While still used in some agricultural enterprises, the great growth of the horse industry has been for recreational and human development purposes. Joe has put together a Handbook for today's horse owners that is easy and enjoyable reading but could also serve as a reference in college classes.

Joe and I met and developed a long time friendship through our careers in developing horse programs at the college level – Joe at New Mexico State in Las Cruces, New Mexico, and myself at Texas A&M University in College Station, Texas. We met at AQHA and other horse breed judging clinics, and each of us developed and managed horse judging programs, horsemanship schools and state 4-H horse shows. We were in the early days

B.F. Yeates and SPOOK

of formal education about horses and shared stories and experiences. We also shared the experiences of raising our children with horses. I developed a great respect for Joe, and the times we spent visiting and working in mutual programs are cherished.

Joe Armstrong has spent a career living with horses and, as an educator, has greatly contributed to the growth of the horse industry. He has put together a great handbook that is well illustrated and is a combination of both scientific and practical information that can be used as a reference throughout the horse industry. I strongly recommend this Handbook to current and future horse owners.

Thank you, Joe, for putting this book together. The practice of using "Thumb Rules" to highlight important truths is unique and helpful. Each time I review a section, I find another "pearl of information" that I had originally overlooked. The following pages contain valuable knowledge that could only come from a lifetime of experiences.

B.F. Yeates
Extension Horse Specialist Emeritus, Texas A&M University
AQHA Hall of Fame
Texas Tech Rodeo Hall of Fame

PREFACE

Writing the HORSEMAN'S HANDBOOK has been a journey. My original intent was to write a comprehensive, practical book for horse owners that would make horse ownership a marvelous experience while helping the new owner avoid the pitfalls and discouragements that go with having to "learn it all on your own".

My dear friend David Whitaker graciously read the manuscript and nailed me: "Joe Armstrong didn't write this book, he lived it! He and son Edward just recorded what happened."

This book shows me how I have been blessed. For me, to be blessed is to be Divinely Favored. I was born in 1937 to strong, loving parents who saw to it that I received a fine education and told me to choose my vocation. I was definitely favored in finding Rusty, convincing her to marry me in 1963, putting up with me, and for being given incredible children and grandchildren, both biological and adopted.

If you are not mentioned in this book, it does not mean that you were not a partner in my journey. Thank you for riding beside me and giving me wisdom and encouragement.

This book is dedicated to my son, Edward Russ. I wrote it, but Ed did the heavy lifting: editing, pictures, illustrations, etc. Thank you, son, for pushing me over the finish line.

Enjoy Your Ride, and may you always ride a good horse!

Joe B. Armstrong

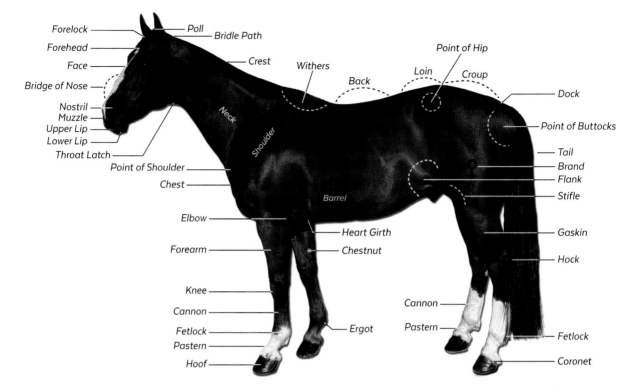

RANKINS REMINIC – 13 year-old Quarter Horse gelding

AUTHOR'S NOTE:

RANKINS REMINIC is my personal riding horse. He was bred by and named for one of my best friends, Bobby Rankin, by one of my best stallions: VON REMINIC. His versatility is illustrated numerous times throughout the pages of this book – from trail riding to working cows, from the show arena to carrying a U.S. Congresswoman – you'll see many pictures of him being enjoyed by myself, my wife Rusty, our children, grandchildren and friends.

Examples and recommendations in this book reference a horse like him: a well-bred, healthy, aged gelding who weighs approximately 1,200 pounds.

His pedigree, kind disposition, training and correct conformation are testaments to the importance of the topics that will be discussed in this book. If so inclined, I hope you can find one like him.

TABLE OF CONTENTS

J.H.B. "Josh" Armstrong, Jr. & RANKINS REMINIC packing into the Pecos Wilderness, NM

INTRODUCTION

The HORSEMAN'S HANDBOOK is meant to be your guidebook; what you really need to know, immediately at your fingertips. As your thirst for additional technical information grows, you will go to highly specific books and videos on nutrition, training, breeding, histories of the horse, etc.

Seminars, short courses and clinics are wonderful for expanding your knowledge and for getting different opinions.

> **"Guidebooks merely describe the skeleton, leaving the memory to clothe it with romance."** – *Arnold Lunn*

In some regards this book may seem somewhat backwards in its contents since it starts with:

PART 1 – **Obligations Of Ownership**, followed by

PART 2 – **Purchasing Your Horse** and

PART 3 – **Now You Own Your Horse** then

PART 4 – **Riding Your Horse** and finally

PART 4 – **Reproduction**

I feel it is crucial that you know what you are getting into when you take on horse ownership. Time, attention, facilities, lifestyle, friends, etc. are equally important as finances. Ownership and involvement may mean that you will drop older friendships and take on new friends who share your horse interests. It may also change your lifestyle and recreation. The changes can be exciting, long lasting and extremely gratifying as you give your horse involvement the TLC it requires. This could be the greatest adventure of your life – go for it! Just remember from the beginning:

The purchase price of the horse is the tip of the iceberg!

This will become clearer as you read on.

Photo ©SZ Photo / Scherl/Bridgeman Images

"You cannot love a car the way you love a horse. The horse brings out human feelings the way machines cannot do."

—*Albert Einstein*

October 11, 1933, Cromer, Norfolk County, England — Einstein, the brilliant physicist and Nobel laureate, near the vacation home of British Naval Commander Oliver Locker Lampson (horseback aboard GOLDEN BOY) with two of Einstein's secretaries, Betty Goodall and M. Howard, armed for his personal protection at the request of Commander Lampson.

Broodmares out to pasture at the Willow Creek Ranch at the Hole-In-The-Wall, Kaycee, WY

Part 1

OBLIGATIONS OF OWNERSHIP

Horse ownership is a wonderful privilege and as with most privileges it invokes responsibility. Responsibility is good for every human being. It serves to bring out the best in us as we reach deep within to do those things which we know must be done and often they can only be done by you.

Ownership and responsibility do not have to be complicated and burdensome. A proper understanding of the horse can make the responsibility of ownership fun and exciting.

The horse is one of God's most magnificent creations. Pictures of horses have existed throughout history. It has been rightly said that "wherever we find civilizations we find the hoof prints of horses". The horse has been used for war, conquests, work and pleasure. Volumes have been written about the debt we owe the noble horse in our existence.

The horse as we know him today is said to be domesticated. Yet the basic self-preservation instinct of the horse remains *flight or fight*. We, too, exhibit much of this same survival instinct. With domestication, an understanding of behavior, training principles, and experience, the horse we enjoy today is a phenomenal athlete and companion.

Breeding programs developed by "saddle seat geneticists" have been extremely successful. More will be discussed regarding different breeding programs, their purposes and successes later. The important fact is that they have produced horses that can be wonderfully used for any equine discipline.

Photo ©AKG-Images

"Don't give your son money. As far as you can afford it, give him horses...No hour of life is lost that is spent in the saddle."

—Sir Winston Churchill

September 1, 1950 – Sir Winston Churchill & Jockey Tommy Gosling celebrate COLONIST II's win in the Florizel Handicap Stakes at Kempton Park Racecourse, in Sunbury-on-Thames, Surrey, England. COLONIST II (TB), a French-bred gray stallion, was Churchill's most successful racehorse. Running under pink silks, COLONIST II won 13 out of 23 races and placed in the money in 5 other races, with total purse earnings of $36,400 ($463,400 in 2023 dollars) before retiring to stud at Newchapel Green.

Georgia Criss Armstrong & her 24 year-old pardner – SAN SOMEBODY

Part 2

PURCHASING YOUR HORSE

Hopefully you are familiar with different horse breeds, the shows and events in which each breed excels and the kind of people that are attracted to each breed.

There is an old saying that Thoroughbreds (racing) are based on old family fortunes, Arabians on the get rich lately, doctors, lawyers and movie stars, and Quarter Horses on West Texas oil and gas. There used to be substantial truth to this adage but today we have many more breeds and specific performance events within each breed. Horse import/export has become common place and there are hundreds of new avenues available to the new horse owner.

Once you have researched breeds and activities, events, opportunities and social involvement, and have decided that you have the desire, time and money to become a horse owner, things become very serious.

> ✌ *Thumb Rule:* **Choose Wisely – the Purchase Price of the Horse is the Tip of the Iceberg**

Linda, Joe III, Eddie, Georgia & Josh Armstrong riding in the Rio Grande Riverbed

YOUR EXPERIENCE AND/OR ABILITY LEVEL

This value must be honestly evaluated and determined. Are you a rank beginner? Did you ride as a youth but have not ridden for several years? Do you have physical or psychological issues (horses are great for each of these when used properly)? Are you athletic and push the envelope or are you passive? Are you currently a rider? Do you currently show or wish to show on a competitive basis?

To purchase a horse that is substantially above your level or one that is completely below your skill level will keep you in a state of frustration.

> ❷ *Thumb Rule:* **Be honest with yourself concerning your ability level**

If you don't know the exact answer to your level then try to ride with friends in different activities and ask them for their honest evaluation of your potential as a rider.

Try out several horses. Don't fall for the first one simply because you are anxious to become a horse owner.

> ❷ *Thumb Rule:* **Haste makes waste**

A PLACE

You must have a place arranged for your horse. This can be your own property or you can rent or lease a stall and/or pen at a professional horse boarding facility. More on horse care and needs will be discussed in Part 3.

Horses grazing in the pasture at Armstrong Equine Service in La Mesa, New Mexico

ADVISOR, AGENT, PROFESSIONAL, CONFIDANT

You need an experienced horse person to serve as your advisor and confidant. The person you choose to help you find the right horse needs to be involved in the discipline in which you're interested. In other words, don't get a Quarter Horse Western Pleasure person to help you find a proper Dressage horse. The horse industry is highly specialized today, so take advantage of experienced professionals who are experts in your chosen area of interest.

The fee for the professional's service is generally 10% of the horse's final purchase price. You may have a friend with expertise who will assist you for free because they are anxious for you to join them in horses. Just be certain that he or she is a thoroughly qualified horseman – no need to ruin a good friendship!

This 10% invested in the right professional may be the least expensive and most important money that you will invest in the long run. Too many people as they begin their horse search go off on their own or solicit advice from people who are not really knowledgeable enough about the entire horse ownership spectrum. This often ends up with the new horse owner paying too much money for a horse that does not fit their needs. They then end up dissatisfied, have invested poorly and either ① sell out and stay out of their envisioned horse ownership or ② they re-group, find experienced help, and start over with a lot more experience and knowledge – and less money.

It doesn't have to be this way if you plan correctly from the start. That 10% fee would have been an excellent investment.

I am constantly amused at how many highly successful businessmen enter the livestock industry without applying the same principles that made their businesses successful.

There's the old and often told scenario about "the man with money comes to the trainer with experience and says he wants experience. Soon the trainer has the money and the money man has the experience!"

    ❷ *Thumb Rule:* **Paying for good professional advice avoids pitfalls**

BREED, REGISTERED OR GRADE

Breed is important because horses of certain breeds are known to be superior in certain disciplines and events.

Breed Registries have the responsibility of maintaining the records for their specific breed. The breed registry creates registration certificates for each horse born within the breed, transfers ownership when a horse is sold to a new owner, and promotes the breed and breed activities. The pedigrees maintained by the various breed registries provide a complete genealogy for each breed.

Horses that have a registration certificate are said to be **registered**. Some people mistakenly refer to any registered horse as a "thoroughbred". This is incorrect because the Thoroughbred is a breed of its own.

A **Grade** horse is not registered and therefore does not enjoy the privileges of the breed association. Being a Grade doesn't mean that the horse is inferior, it simply indicates that it does not belong to any breed registry and therefore is not eligible to participate in shows or activities that are restricted to horses of a specific breed registry.

Some horses are Grades because their owners failed to complete the required paperwork to register the horse in its breed within the required age limit or because the paperwork was lost, destroyed, or never followed through. At some point in time it becomes impossible or financially impractical to register a horse, and it remains a Grade horse for life. Others are Grade because one or both of their parents were Grade, or they are the result of crossing two breeds and neither breed registry accepts that particular cross.

A Grade horse can generally be purchased for less money than a registered horse. It should be noted that it costs the same to stable, feed and transport the Grade but you do not have the same opportunities available with the Grade horse. If you only want a good hunting or riding horse, a Grade may be right up your alley. When you go to sell your Grade it will probably sell for less than a comparable registered horse.

GELDING, MARE OR STALLION

GELDING

Most new owners will get along better with a gelding. The gelding is a castrated male and because he has less hormonal influence, he will generally be easier to handle and perform the same every day. Geldings are considered to be more steady and solid in their daily temperament and work. Most ranches prefer geldings for their remudas.

MARE

Mares have the disadvantage that every 21-22 days they come into heat (estrus). This is the period of time when they are sexually receptive to the stallion. When in estrus, some mares have a totally different personality, are difficult to be around, don't show well, do not get along with other horses, and can be quite "witchy".

All mares do not exhibit this extreme behavior when in estrus. Many show very little abnormal behavior. Hormone therapy is available to lessen this activity for showing, etc. A major advantage of purchasing a mare is that she can be bred and raise foals should she become crippled or unable to perform, even if for only a year or so (more about this on page 169).

Gregor Mendel's original genetic principle is "Like produces like", so be sure your mare is qualified to be a mother!

> ❷ *Thumb Rule:* **Inferior mares should not be allowed to reproduce**

Foal: Baby horse
Filly: Female foal
Colt: Male foal
Weanling: Less than one year old that has been weaned from its mother
Yearling: 1 year old (as of January 1st on the year after its birth)
Gelding: Male that has been castrated and cannot breed
Mare: Mature adult female
Brood Mare: Mare that is primarily used for breeding
Stallion: Mature adult male, typically used for breeding

The author with a young Thoroughbred racehorse stallion, PLATINUM PHAROAH

STALLION

I don't have the answer! Too many people seem to want to start their horse ownership with a *two-year-old stallion*. Nothing can be more aggravating or dangerous for the new horse owner with limited experience. Stallions demand constant attention and scrutiny. Some bite, paw, kick, squeal and generally act like misguided teenagers, especially when not properly disciplined. In the hands of experienced horsemen, stallions are acceptable and may be worth a lot of money. The new horse owner should stay away from a stallion unless you intend to immediately have the veterinarian geld (castrate) your stallion. Once gelded, it will take two or more months for most to lose this stallion behavior and take on the temperament of a gelding.

Stallion prospects have the potential advantage that they may have nicer conformation than many geldings. The main issue is to have the stallion gelded and let time pass before the new owner takes daily care of the new gelding. Don't hesitate to castrate. If anyone asks me if they should geld their stallion my standard answer without even seeing their horse is "**yes**".

> ❷ *Thumb Rule:* **It takes a good stallion to make a great gelding**

COLOR

Color is strictly in the eye of the beholder. Just as with different breeds, there are great horses of all colors. Be sure the horse is conformationally sound, of good disposition, etc., as well as the color you decide on. Some breeds such as Palomino and Buckskin are restricted to horses of a specific color. Palominos and Buckskins may also be registered Quarter Horses depending on their parents' breed. Every breed publishes a book of rules and regulations that will answer all of your questions concerning color.

2022 AQHA REGISTRATIONS BY COLOR

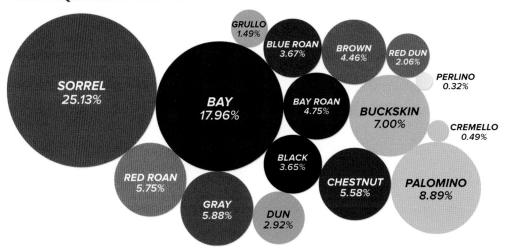

Source: Courtesy of the American Quarter Horse Association – https://aqha.com

To say that the science of color is complicated is an understatement! Two pigments, black (eumelanin) and red (pheomelanin), form the varying shades of the basic coat colors: black, bay (black + red) and chestnut (red). Other genetic modifiers, dilutions and white patterns expand these colors into the vast array of horse colorations that are unique to each individual.

Names used to describe coat colors and patterns vary between associations but are generally based on a combination of the phenotype (colors appearing on the body and **points** – the mane, tail, ear rims and lower legs) and the genotype (inherited DNA). The following page shows some of the commonly used names for the basic colors, dilutions and white patterns.

☺ *Thumb Rule:* Always ride a good horse regardless of his color

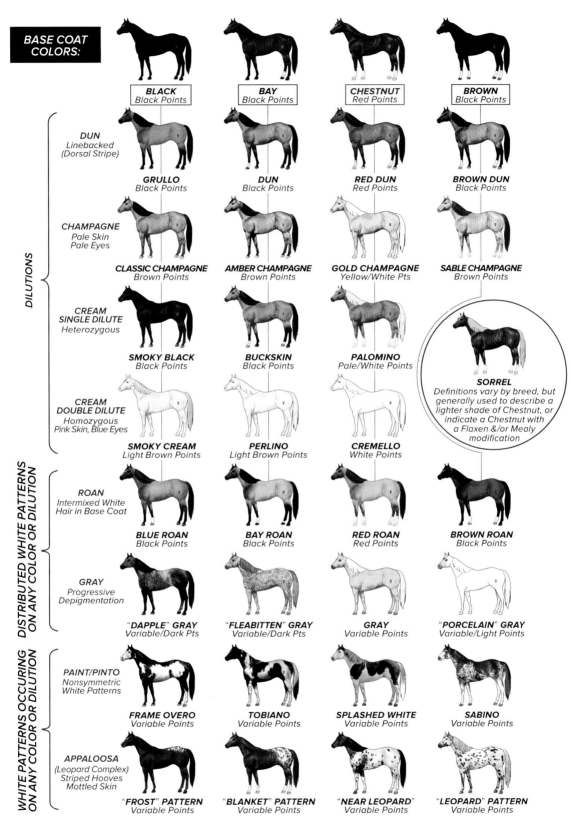

BASE COAT COLORS:

BLACK *Black Points* | **BAY** *Black Points* | **CHESTNUT** *Red Points* | **BROWN** *Black Points*

DILUTIONS

DUN *Linebacked (Dorsal Stripe)*
- **GRULLO** *Black Points*
- **DUN** *Black Points*
- **RED DUN** *Red Points*
- **BROWN DUN** *Black Points*

CHAMPAGNE *Pale Skin Pale Eyes*
- **CLASSIC CHAMPAGNE** *Brown Points*
- **AMBER CHAMPAGNE** *Brown Points*
- **GOLD CHAMPAGNE** *Yellow/White Pts*
- **SABLE CHAMPAGNE** *Brown Points*

CREAM SINGLE DILUTE *Heterozygous*
- **SMOKY BLACK** *Black Points*
- **BUCKSKIN** *Black Points*
- **PALOMINO** *Pale/White Points*

CREAM DOUBLE DILUTE *Homozygous Pink Skin, Blue Eyes*
- **SMOKY CREAM** *Light Brown Points*
- **PERLINO** *Light Brown Points*
- **CREMELLO** *White Points*

SORREL *Definitions vary by breed, but generally used to describe a lighter shade of Chestnut, or indicate a Chestnut with a Flaxen &/or Mealy modification*

DISTRIBUTED WHITE PATTERNS ON ANY COLOR OR DILUTION

ROAN *Intermixed White Hair in Base Coat*
- **BLUE ROAN** *Black Points*
- **BAY ROAN** *Black Points*
- **RED ROAN** *Red Points*
- **BROWN ROAN** *Black Points*

GRAY *Progressive Depigmentation*
- **"DAPPLE" GRAY** *Variable/Dark Pts*
- **"FLEABITTEN" GRAY** *Variable/Dark Pts*
- **GRAY** *Variable Points*
- **"PORCELAIN" GRAY** *Variable/Light Points*

WHITE PATTERNS OCCURING ON ANY COLOR OR DILUTION

PAINT/PINTO *Nonsymmetric White Patterns*
- **FRAME OVERO** *Variable Points*
- **TOBIANO** *Variable Points*
- **SPLASHED WHITE** *Variable Points*
- **SABINO** *Variable Points*

APPALOOSA *(Leopard Complex) Striped Hooves Mottled Skin*
- **"FROST" PATTERN** *Variable Points*
- **"BLANKET" PATTERN** *Variable Points*
- **"NEAR LEOPARD"** *Variable Points*
- **"LEOPARD" PATTERN** *Variable Points*

Some other colors not pictured: Seal Brown – a Brown Base Coat with a Sooty (or Pangaré) Modification, Silver Dilutes, Pearl Dilutes, Mushroom Dilutes, Dominant White or White Spotting & other patterns. Reference: Sponenberg DP, Bellone, R. 2017. Equine Color Genetics 4th Ed. John Wiley & Sons, Inc.

WHITE MARKINGS ON THE HEAD & LEGS

White markings on the face and legs commonly occur in nearly every breed. The genetics are not yet well understood, but it is observable that chestnuts generally have more expansive markings than bays, and bays more than blacks.

Face markings are named by the extent of their size and location and can additionally be described as narrow, faint, disconnected, irregular, etc. The following lists describe some of the commonly used names:

- **Star** – white marking on the forehead
- **Strip** – narrow white marking running vertically over the nasal bone
- **Snip** – white marking on the muzzle between the nostrils
- **Stripe** – white marking indicating a connected Star, Strip & Snip
- **Race** – asymmetric stripe that runs off to the side of the face
- **Chin Spots** – white markings on the lower lip
- **Blaze** – broad vertical white marking extending the length of the face
- **Bald Face** – very broad blaze; typically encompassing the eyes and extending down around the nostrils & lips (muzzle), and sides of face

STAR	STAR, STRIP & SNIP		BLAZE	BALD FACE
WIMPY	**DOC BAR**	**SECRETARIAT**	**DASH FOR CASH**	**GUNNER**
AQHA #0000001	AQHA #0076136	TB #Z20669	AQHA #1238058	APHA #0271197
Star – white mark on the forehead	*DOC BAR has a Star with disconnected Stripe (or Race) & Snip. SECRETARIAT has a Star-Strip-Snip that could also be described as a Star & narrow Stripe albeit a disconnected Snip*		*Blaze – broad stripe extending the length of the face, to the bottom of his upper lip*	*Bald Face – white extends around the eyes down over the muzzle & sides of face with blue eyes*

Images based on paintings by AQHA Hall of Fame Member Orren Mixer: https://www.aqha.com/-/orren-mixer

Leg markings are named by the upper most extent of their reach on a limb.

- **Partial Heel** – white on the inside or outside bulb the of heel, or
- **Heel** – white on the entire heel
- **Coronet** – white just above the hoof covering the coronary band
- **Half Pastern** – white extending halfway up to the pastern
- **Pastern** – white extending to the top of the pastern
- **Fetlock** (or Ankle) – white extending up to the top of the fetlock
- **Sock** (or Half Cannon) – white extending halfway up the cannon bone
- **3/4 Stocking** (or Cannon) – white extending to top of the cannon bone
- **Stocking** (or Hock) – white extending up to the hock/knee
- **High White** (or Above Hock) – white extending above the hock/knee
- **Distal Spots** – small white spots on the coronary band
- **Ermine Spots** – dark spots in white markings just above the hoof

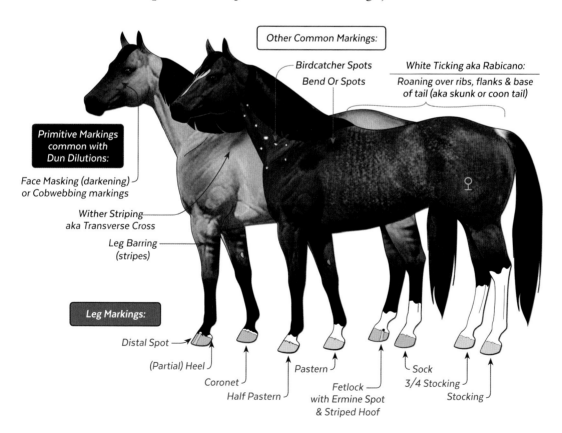

Other Common Markings:

Birdcatcher Spots
Bend Or Spots

White Ticking aka Rabicano:
Roaning over ribs, flanks & base
of tail (aka skunk or coon tail)

Primitive Markings
common with
Dun Dilutions:

Face Masking (darkening)
or Cobwebbing markings

Wither Striping
aka Transverse Cross

Leg Barring
(stripes)

Leg Markings:

Distal Spot

(Partial) Heel

Coronet

Half Pastern

Pastern

Fetlock
with Ermine Spot
& Striped Hoof

Sock
3/4 Stocking

Stocking

Lew Sterrett & HANSOME ponying COMO SE GUNNER at a Sermon On The Mount presentation

AGE

Age is a little like the two-year-old stallion. The young horse is a poor choice for the new owner that is a beginner, novice, older or disabled. The owner should look for a gelding or mare that is somewhere between 8-16 years of age. Horses in this age range are generally well trained, settled, and will be the same day to day. If not ridden for a week or two they will not try to buck you off. This age horse should have several good years ahead.

It is important to realize that for most, your first horse will not be your last. As you get ready for a new, younger horse, your now older horse should be ideal for the next new horse owner. They will probably provide the same TLC that you gave him. Older geldings make great kids horses. As you become a more proficient rider, you may decide to buy a younger prospect to train and bring along as a replacement while you enjoy your older horse. Don't fall for the two-year-old.

❷ *Thumb Rule:* Age in a sound horse is an asset

Photo ©Caryn Hill Photography

Trainer Mike Tougas & VON MORE ROUND showing in Reining in Albuquerque, NM

TRAINING

The amount of good training that your prospect has will influence the price. You'll notice that I said **good training**. Good training is worth what you have to pay for it. Poor training actually takes value away from your prospect. Some horses never overcome the damage of poor training in their early development. The first 30-60 days of a horse's training may be the most important! Training fees generally range from $500 to $1,500 per month. This fee normally includes feed and board during training but not farrier and veterinary expenses. Most older horses are not priced with all of their previous training costs.

Purchasing a well trained, older horse is the preferred way to go – you can enjoy the instant gratification of horse ownership. This is where your professional agent or advisor can be your greatest asset. The prospect needs to be ridden by you to be certain that the two of you are a match.

❷ *Thumb Rule:* **Poor training is worse than no training**

CONFORMATION

The horse's conformation is his form, shape, structural correctness, and balance. You'll notice the word is conform, not confirm. Proper conformation not only dictates the horse's beauty and a certain amount of his ability to be a great athlete but also his ability to stay sound. Soundness is extremely important for the equine athlete. A sound horse is always ready to perform. An unsound horse is a burden financially and may not be able to be ridden and enjoyed, although he still costs money every day.

GENERAL CONFORMATION

Symmetry – Taller horses have longer bones! Balance is the criterion. While not exact, the length of the neck, shoulder, back and hip should be similar. The more forward slope that the shoulder has, the longer the horse's underline will be. The longer underline initiates a longer stride and allows more room

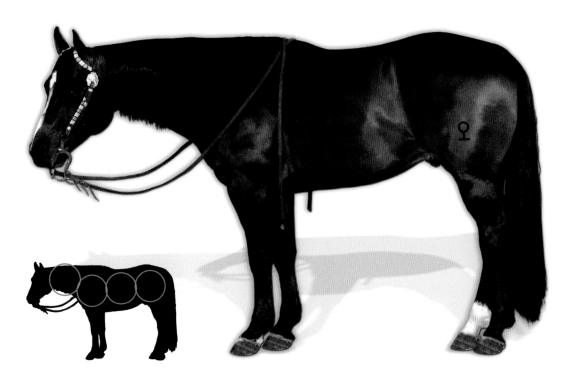

VON REMINIC, National Reining Horse Association (NRHA) Open Futurity Champion, typifies the balance & conformation desirable in performance horses. As a yearling in 1998 VON REMINIC was the highest priced yearling ever sold in a NRHA Futurity Sale

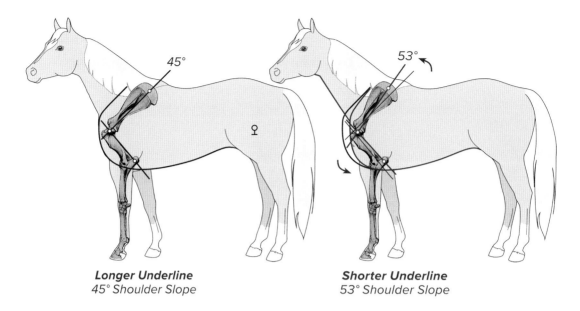

Longer Underline
45° Shoulder Slope

Shorter Underline
53° Shoulder Slope

in the area where the cinch goes. The horse should have a well-defined wither to make it easier to keep the saddle in place with less cinch pressure. The horse's height is measured from the top of the withers to the ground in "hands", with 1 hand equal to 4 inches.

Head – The head needs to be proportional in size to the horse's body. A pretty head is desired because it is generally the first thing you see. There are certain characteristics that are generally accepted as desirable – just remember "beauty is in the eye of the beholder". That said, we like a reasonably short, flat face with a prominent eye sitting out on the corner.

Many people consider the eye to be an indicator of disposition. A small, sunken, almond shaped eye is called a **pig eye** and is often thought to indicate meanness. Many pig eyed horses are also **roman nosed**. It is quite possible that this perceived meanness is due to the fact that these horses physically cannot see as well. The horse described in the popular song *The Strawberry Roan*, written by Curley Fletcher, was said to have "little pig eyes and a big roman nose"! There are horses that have lost one eye and go on to make fine performance horses. But two eyes are better than one.

Throat Latch – A clean throat latch makes it easier for the horse to flex at the poll and be a more supple athlete.

Teeth – When you part the horse's lips the teeth should make occlusional contact. If the upper incisors extend forward of the lower incisors as much

Correct

Overshot

Undershot

as the thickness of a credit card the horse is **parrot mouthed** or **overshot**. If the lowers extend past the uppers he is called **monkey mouthed** or **undershot**. A small degree of either will not prevent the horse from being a fine athlete. If either condition is extreme the horse might not be able to survive on poor pasture or desert conditions because he may not be able to physically harvest enough grass to maintain himself. However, the way we feed most horses in the U.S., these horses will stay fat and make good athletes.

The major problem is the fact that these dental conditions are considered **genetic defects** that are transmissible to future generations. In halter or conformation classes at most horse shows these conditions result in stallions and mares (but not geldings) being disqualified from the class. This is to prevent the increase of this genetic defect from being perpetuated in future generations. Insist on optimum conformation and soundness in a horse that is attractive to you.

❷ *Thumb Rule:* You'll never find perfect conformation

Conformation and soundness are areas that your professional or expert can be of great assistance. The prospective horse purchase needs to be scrutinized all over, but especially from his knees and hocks to the ground. We will never have a horse with perfect conformation. We can, however, use proper selection criteria to minimize soundness problems. I emphasize structure from the knees and hocks down to the ground because these areas are basically analogous to the stability structures – wheels and tires – on your automobile. You don't want to drive your automobile at high speeds with your family and friends when the tie rods are loose, the camber is off, the tires are out of balance and the tread is no good. The same goes for the riding horse. He needs to be strong, correct and well tuned.

Million Dollar Rider Todd Sommers & VON REMINIC — NRHA Futurity winners, earning $180,219 in 2000 while setting the record as the All Time Leading Money Earning Reining Horse. An elite athlete, VON REMINIC's soundness is a testament to proper conformation

FRONT LEG

The average horse carries 60% of his weight on his front end when moving forward at the walk. The column of bones from the point of the shoulder through the knee, ankle and hoof should be straight. If the knees are outside of this vertical line the horse is **bowlegged**. Bowleggedness puts extreme pressure on the inside portion of the knee and tends to become worse with age. When the knees are inside the vertical line we call the condition **in at the knees** and more pressure is exerted on the outside of the knees. Both of these situations need to be avoided at all cost. Mark these horses off your prospect list.

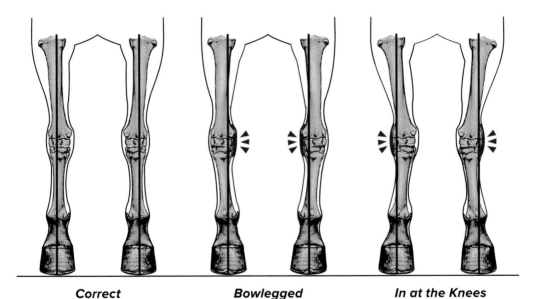

Correct   **Bowlegged**   **In at the Knees**

Knee – Starting with a view from the front, the knees can be construed as analogous to the headlights of your automobile. The knees should face straight ahead. The knee is made of eight cuboidical bones that articulate upon each other as the horse moves forward or backward. It is important that the vertical and lateral pressures on these bones be uniformly distributed in order to prevent bone chips, fractures and other injuries.

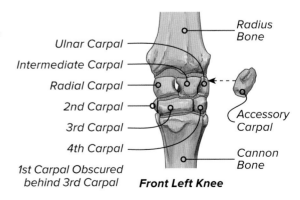

Radius Bone

Ulnar Carpal

Intermediate Carpal

Radial Carpal

2nd Carpal

3rd Carpal

4th Carpal

Accessory Carpal

Cannon Bone

1st Carpal Obscured behind 3rd Carpal

Front Left Knee

When viewed from the side, the knees should also be straight. If the knees are behind a vertical line down the side of the leg the horse is said to be **back at the knee** or **calf-kneed**. This condition is extremely detrimental because, as the horse is in forward motion, the edges of the cube-shaped bones in the knee will interfere with each other and create bone chips. You will have a crippled horse that may require surgery, and even after surgery, is not a good candidate for soundness.

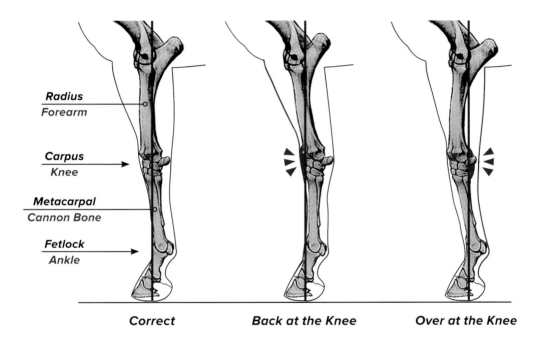

Radius		
Forearm		
Carpus		
Knee		
Metacarpal		
Cannon Bone		
Fetlock		
Ankle		

Correct   **Back at the Knee**   **Over at the Knee**

Drop the horse that is back at the knee from your prospect list. Odds are, he will cost you major veterinary expenses and keep you disappointed.

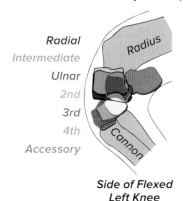

Radial
Intermediate
Ulnar
2nd
3rd
4th
Accessory

Radius

Cannon

Side of Flexed Left Knee

The horse that has his knee slightly forward of the vertical line is said to be **over at the knee** or **buck kneed**. This condition is more unsightly but is much less obtrusive than the back at the knee syndrome. The horse that is slightly over at the knee has more room to articulate as he moves. Straight is desired, but over is conformationally much better than back at the knee.

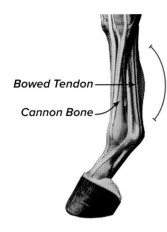

Bowed Tendon

Cannon Bone

Tendon – When viewed from the side, the tendon that runs down the leg directly behind the knee and cannon bone and attaches to the coffin bone inside the hoof should appear smooth, full and strong. Horses that have had a torn or traumatized tendon will generally have a bowed image when viewed from the side. The general rule is to stay away from a horse that has a **bowed tendon**. Some horses return to full athletic activity after a bow, but the odds are against you.

Cannon Bone – The cannon bone is the large bone extending from the knee or hock to the ankle. This bone should be of good diameter, and while it is actually round, it should give the appearance from the side of being almost flat because of the tendons running behind and in front of the bone. The cannon bone should be as short as possible relative to the other long bones. A horse with short cannon bones (front and rear legs) is said to have his "knees and hocks close to the ground". This gives an advantage in leverage for speed, stops, turns and jumping.

Rusty Armstrong & RANKINS REMINIC light on their toes sorting corriente cattle at Josh's La Union Ranch, La Union, New Mexico

A horse may have a **splint** on the cannon bone (see page 36). Splints normally occur on the inside of the cannon bones and are ossifications or calcifications due to injury or trauma. Unless splints are up at the knee where they may interfere with normal knee function (some can be surgically removed), they are considered only **blemishes** – not faults.

Pastern – When viewed from the side, the pastern – the bones between the ankle and the hoof – should be moderate in length and have about a 45° angle with the ground. Don't get carried away with the angles; just be sure that the angles in the front limb are harmonious or balanced. The angle of the pastern and the horse's shoulder angle are generally similar. These angles are largely responsible for the softness in the horse's stride. They are the auto's shock absorbers. If the pastern and shoulder angles are somewhat straight the ride will be rough, just like your auto when the shocks are worn out and need replacing. The too straight horse is a candidate for soundness problems, especially **navicular disease**.

The horse that has too much slope or angle in the pastern will be more pronc to tendon problems. The angles of the pastern and the hoof wall should also be analogous.

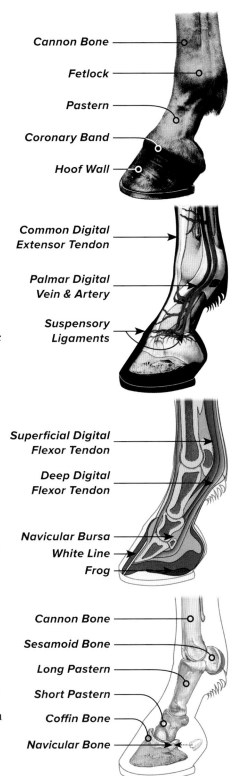

Cannon Bone
Fetlock
Pastern
Coronary Band
Hoof Wall

Common Digital Extensor Tendon
Palmar Digital Vein & Artery
Suspensory Ligaments

Superficial Digital Flexor Tendon
Deep Digital Flexor Tendon
Navicular Bursa
White Line
Frog

Cannon Bone
Sesamoid Bone
Long Pastern
Short Pastern
Coffin Bone
Navicular Bone

Images adapted from Hermann Dittrich's Das Pferd, Tafel 15
https://digital.library.wisc.edu/1711.dl/LUKJILKN3GOBS83 (8/2023)

25

Megan Schuller & POINT AND SHOOT displaying fancy footwork turning a cow down the fence in Working Cow Horse at the SWQHA Futurity in Las Cruces, NM

Hoof – The hoof is extremely important because it is the object that makes contact with the ground every time a foot is moved. Imagine the impact when a horse is running full speed (see page 100) and then suddenly stops or turns and charges off in the other direction!

The shape of the front hooves should be round. The rear hooves will tend to be a very slight bit oval and smaller than the front hooves. The size of the hoof should be in direct proportion to the size of the horse. There are three bones within the hoof capsule. The hoof needs to be solid and not flaky because it must hold the horseshoe solidly in place during extreme performance as well as absorb impact.

Front Hoof

When viewed from the side, the angle of the hoof wall and the pastern should be the same. The outer wall of the hoof should be smooth. When a horse undergoes an extreme change in nutrition, it can be detected in the character of the hoof wall below the **coronary band**. The coronary band is the hairy structure at the top of the hoof. This is where hoof growth begins (similar to your cuticle). It takes about one year to grow an entirely new hoof.

Rear Hoof

An extreme nutritional change will result in a different texture running laterally around the hoof; this is not a problem if it merely indicates a nutritional change has taken place. However, if there are a series of rings on the hoof wall, this may be an indication that the horse has been foundered in the past. **Founder** is the common term for **laminitis**. Past founder indicates that the horse may have permanent foot and soundness damage and/or that he will be predisposed to future founder.

Foundered Hoof Wall

Rings and slumping hoof wall characteristic of Founder (Laminitis disease)

Some founder cases are mild, but many are horrific and often, after much expense, result in the horse having to be euthanized. If you have any question about the hooves have your professional, Vet, and/or farrier make a thorough examination for you.

Bottom of Hoof

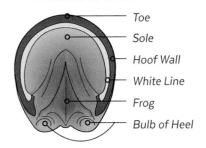

Toe
Sole
Hoof Wall
White Line
Frog
Bulb of Heel

Also study the bottom of the hoof for abnormalities. Just remember, an auto with poor lights, steering, wheels and tires is an accident looking for a place to happen. So is the bad-legged and footed horse.

Foot Movement – Few horses and few people move their feet in a pattern of perfect flight. The horse that **toes-in** or is **pigeon toed** tends to move its feet in a **paddling** motion. The foot goes forward and paddles or moves to the outside as it comes back as the horse's body moves forward over it. I refer to this as looking like a pickup truck coming down the road with the doors open. While the toed-in condition is unsightly, it is a less severe conformational fault than the **toed-out**, **splayed** or **coon footed** condition. The toed-out horse tends to dish the hoof inward as he moves. This winging in or **dishing-in** can result in the hoof interfering with or hitting the other hoof, ankle or cannon bone in the opposite front limb and cause splints and/or temporary or permanent lameness.

If you must choose between these conditions, toed-in is preferable. Remember, the straighter or more correct, the better. These two conditions can often be corrected with proper farrier care very early in the horse's life. The corrective changes need to occur in the first six to twelve months of the horse's life. To try to correct a mature horse would be like putting corrective

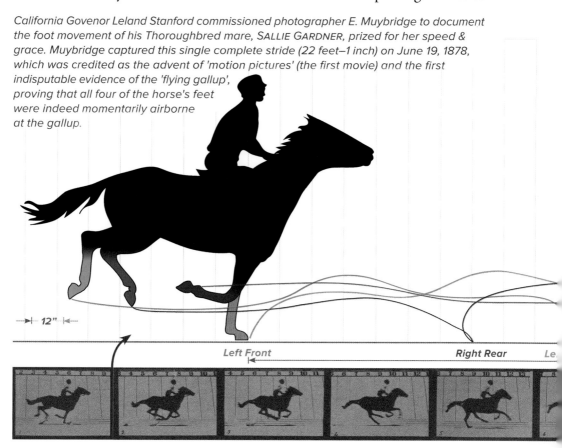

California Govenor Leland Stanford commissioned photographer E. Muybridge to document the foot movement of his Thoroughbred mare, SALLIE GARDNER, prized for her speed & grace. Muybridge captured this single complete stride (22 feet–1 inch) on June 19, 1878, which was credited as the advent of 'motion pictures' (the first movie) and the first indisputable evidence of the 'flying gallup', proving that all four of the horse's feet were indeed momentarily airborne at the gallup.

12"

Left Front   *Right Rear*   *Le*

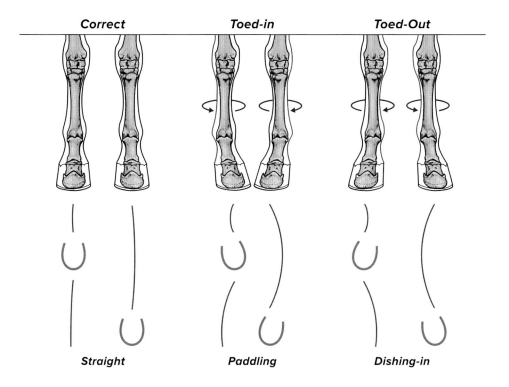

Correct	Toed-in	Toed-Out
Straight	Paddling	Dishing-in

A century later, MIT Professor George Pratt measured SECRETARIAT's stride at 24 ft–4 in, about the average of today's elite race horses. However, SECRETARIAT still holds he record for the fastest average Triple Crown speed with his win in 1973 at 37.7 mph, followed by AFFIRMED in 1978 at 37.0 mph & SEATTLE SLEW in 1977 at 36.8 mph (zarebasystems.com).

A necropsy of SECRETARIAT revealed he had an abnormally large heart, a whopping 22 pounds! Well more than twice the size of an average Thoroughbred (8.5 lbs). Stride distances for slower gaits are commonly thought to be 12 ft at the lope & 4 ft at the trot.

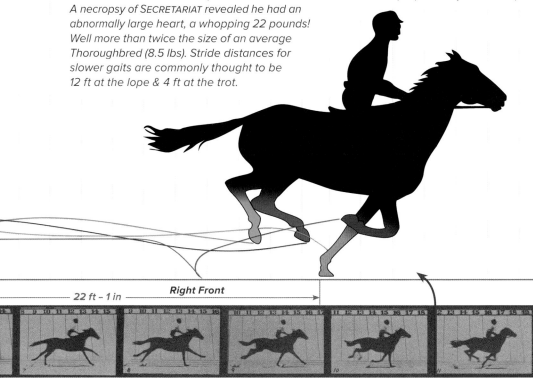

22 ft – 1 in ——— Right Front

Adapted from Eadweard Muybridge – https://www.nga.gov/collection/artist-info.16474.html (8/2023)

shoes on a mature human. The bones are set and the correction will not only hurt the affected problem area but also those joints above or below the intended correction. A mature horse with a slight toe-in or out that does not show signs of interfering, has stayed sound and puts his foot down flat is probably okay; just don't try to change him at this age. Many great equine and human athletes are far from perfect, but proper training and care have enabled them to perform well over a lifetime of competition. The closer you observe movement the more idiosyncrasies you'll notice. Begin to study human athletes and you'll notice that most of your sprinters and scatbacks will tend to be slightly toed-in – that little tidbit is free! The toed-out footballers play on the line and seldom receive their deserved accolades.

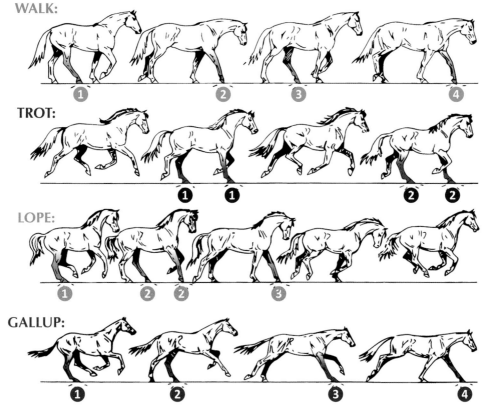

Illustration of Gaits adapted with permission from Alberta 4-H Horse Reference Manual
Source: https://4hab.com/wp-content/uploads/2020/09/Equine-Reference-Manual.pdf Pages 91-92 (8/2023)

❷ **Thumb Rule:** **Slightly toed-in is preferable to toed-out & over at the knee is preferable to back at the knee**

Toed-in but clearly an athlete!

HIND LEG

Today's high performance horses rely on sound hind legs to enable them to stop, turn 180°, jump backwards or sideways and then forward at full speed, only to repeat the same movement a split second later. Reining horses make four or more 360° spins at rapid speed in both directions.

Side View: When viewed from the side the horse's stifle joint is the same as your knee. His hock joint is your ankle. As with the front limb the cannon bone should be short. The hock needs to be reasonably large, clean and appear strong. Angulation of the bones is important. A plumb line dropped from the back of the hip bone to the ground should touch the back of the hock and the ankle. If the hock sticks out behind this line the horse will have difficulty stopping and turning. A prospect with this issue should not be considered for roping, reining, cutting, racing, jumping, etc. He might be okay for western pleasure and trail. Again correctness is preferred. When there is angulation such that the cannon bone and ankle are forward of the vertical line the horse is said to be **sickle hocked**. Many great stopping horses – reiners, cutters and ropers – are slightly sickle hocked. While this condition may aid in the ability to stop it also puts additional stress on the hock. Many sickle hocked horses require monthly or bi-monthly costly injections to keep them sound and performing at a high level.

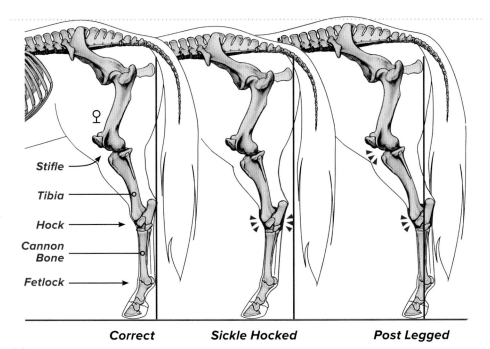

Stifle

Tibia

Hock

Cannon
Bone

Fetlock

Correct *Sickle Hocked* *Post Legged*

The horse whose hocks and ankles are behind the vertical line is said to be **post legged** or **too straight**. This condition generally results in the horse's hips being higher than his withers (increasing weight bearing on his front limbs) and changes all of the angles in the hind limb. Post legged horses have a much higher degree of stifle problems. These problems result in soreness, unsoundness, lack of ability to be used and often require surgery. Many of today's halter horses are too straight in their hocks.

❷ *Thumb Rule:* **Correctness is desired but slightly sickle hocked is preferable to post legged**

Rear View: When viewed from behind our plumb line should bisect the hock, ankle and hoof. Again if the hocks are outside the plumb lines the horse is **bowed** and this is a potentially very bad soundness issue. It will get worse over time. When the hocks are inward of our verticals we call the condition **cow hocked**. While not desirable cow hocked is preferable to bowlegged. Eliminating stress to the hock joint is the object.

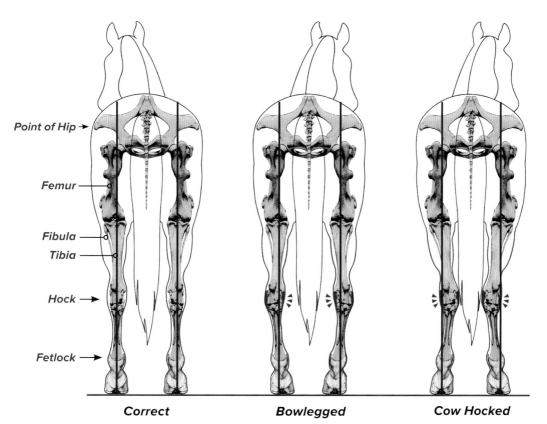

Correct	*Bowlegged*	*Cow Hocked*

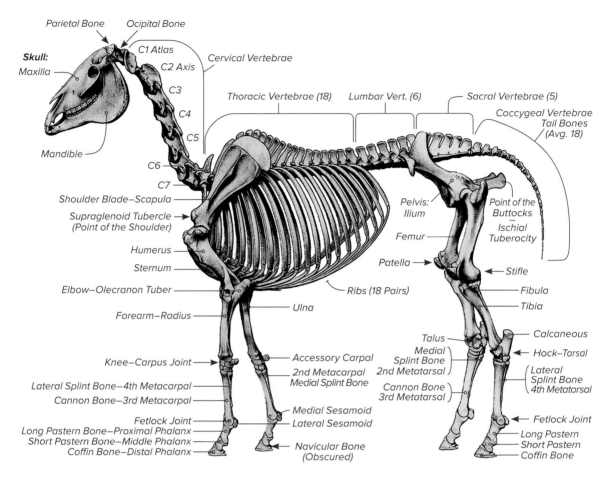

Skeletal System – Image adapted from Herman Dittrich's Das Pferd, Tafel 3
https://digital.library.wisc.edu/1711.dl/OESBV7ZOOJ7JG9A (8/2023)

MUSCULATURE

Earlier we said that conformation is the horse's form, shape, structural correctness and balance. The horse's skeleton is made up of 205 bones. These bones, with their form and shape, have muscles attached to them by tendons. Bones are attached to each other by ligaments.

Some horses, like some people, are heavier muscled than others. Most horses have adequate muscle mass for athletic purposes. The amount, smoothness, and quantity of muscles make a horse's conformation more pleasing or attractive. The musculature, when covered by skin and filled out by body fat, yields our complete horse.

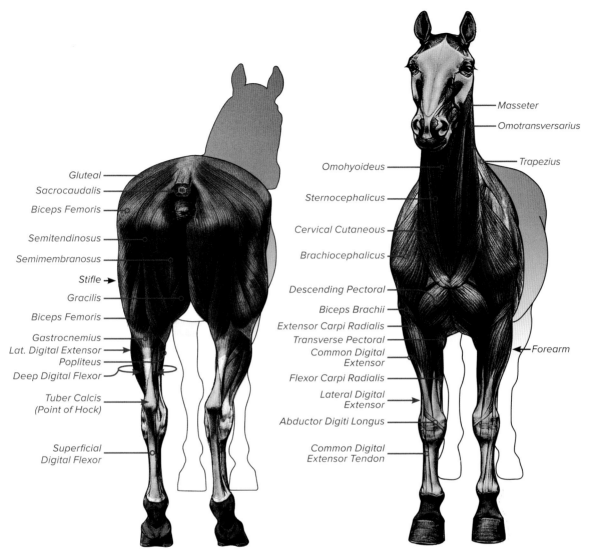

Gluteal
Sacrocaudalis
Biceps Femoris
Semitendinosus
Semimembranosus
Stifle →
Gracilis
Biceps Femoris
Gastrocnemius
Lat. Digital Extensor →
Popliteus
Deep Digital Flexor
Tuber Calcis
(Point of Hock)
Superficial
Digital Flexor

Masseter
Omotransversarius
Trapezius
Omohyoideus
Sternocephalicus
Cervical Cutaneous
Brachiocephalicus
Descending Pectoral
Biceps Brachii
Extensor Carpi Radialis
Transverse Pectoral
Common Digital
Extensor
← Forearm
Flexor Carpi Radialis
Lateral Digital
Extensor
Abductor Digiti Longus
Common Digital
Extensor Tendon

Superficial Musculature – Image adapted from Herman Dittrich's Das Pferd, Tafels 10 & 12
https://digital.library.wisc.edu/1711.dl/GFTO6JALJBVCZ8T (8/2023)

Generally speaking, we believe that long, smooth muscling lends itself more favorably to extreme athletic ability than does short, bunchy muscling.

The inside **forearm** muscle of the front limb is generally considered to be very important for speed since the outside muscles push the limbs forward and the inside muscles pull the limbs back.

The **stifle** area viewed from the rear should be the widest part of a well muscled horse's body. This musculature is largely responsible for powerful starts and stops.

BLEMISHES

Blemishes should not affect the horse's function. Common blemishes are scars and splints. **Splints** generally occur on the inside of the front cannon bones. Splints are ossifications (calcifications) generally due to trauma. The trauma is often a result of a hoof striking the opposite cannon bone. Splints can also occur in young horses as a result of hard exercise on dense surfaces. Splints can be reduced in size if treated early or with surgery. Unless they are high near the knee and cause joint interference, consider splints as unsightly but in most cases harmless. **Scars** are unsightly but unless they cover a joint are generally harmless.

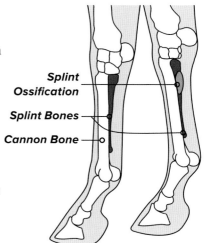

Splint
Ossification

Splint Bones

Cannon Bone

➋ *Thumb Rule:* **Blemishes are normally not soundness issues**

PREPURCHASE VETERINARY EXAM

Especially when purchasing a high-dollar horse, many people desire to have their Vet examine the prospect and give their decision or blessing. This is a good idea, and if the horse will be insured, you're going to need a vet exam and a completed insurance form. Again, be sure your Vet is an equine specialist. You don't want a small animal Vet telling you yes or no on your horse prospect.

You as the potential purchaser are responsible for the cost of this exam. Your Vet will decide whether or not x-rays, etc., are needed; follow their wishes.

On mature horses that have been used and competed on, you will always find something on the x-rays such as minor chips, etc. Discuss these with your Vet and determine if they are truly detrimental to soundness or are something that will probably never be an issue but will always be there on x-ray. I'd hate for my joints to be x-rayed, and I'm sound for the long haul!

➋ *Thumb Rule:* **Soundness exams range greatly in price: $500-$2k**

Josh Armstrong & SUERTE FUERTE chimney-sweeping to Mary Poppin's "Chim-Chim-Cheree" bridleless to win the Freestyle Reining at the Quarter Horse Congress in Columbus, OH – 1991

GENETIC DEFECTS AND UNDESIRABLE TRAITS

Several genetic abnormalities have been discovered or uncovered in the past few years. It would require its own book to fully discuss them. Just be aware that they exist and check with the breed association of your chosen horse as to the diseases and their genetic transmission. The Veterinary Genetics Laboratory at the University of California Davis has been a leader in this research. Fortunately, there are DNA tests for these genetic abnormalities (*https://vgl.ucdavis.edu/species/horse*).

HERDA (*Hereditary Equine Regional Dermal Asthenia*) is one genetic abnormality that is a single gene recessive trait. It demonstrates both the good and bad of line breeding.

HERDA is a skin disorder that is associated primarily with cutting horse pedigrees. Because there is more and more crossover between cutters, reiners, cow horses and ropers, HERDA takes on more significance. HERDA is also a single gene genetic recessive. The gene must come from each parent for it to manifest in the offspring.

Apparently, there is an inability of the collagen to correctly fasten the skin to the musculature, and an injury will result in the skin just falling away.

SKIN TISSUE CROSS SECTION

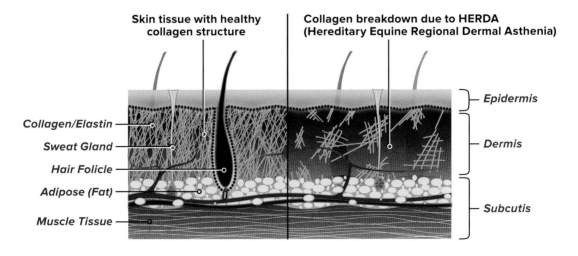

Skin tissue with healthy collagen structure

Collagen breakdown due to **HERDA** (Hereditary Equine Regional Dermal Asthenia)

Collagen/Elastin

Sweat Gland

Hair Follicle

Adipose (Fat)

Muscle Tissue

Epidermis

Dermis

Subcutis

Saddling may do the same. These horses are not able to be ridden because the saddle cannot stay in place and the skin rolls and looks similar to the skin of a Shar-pei dog. There is a DNA test for the HERDA gene. If you are purchasing a mature horse there is no concern unless it is a mare or stallion that may be used for breeding. If purchasing a weanling to two-year-old that has not been ridden and contains cutting bloodlines, it is a good idea to require a negative HERDA DNA test.

Most horse people I talk with at present have never seen a HERDA horse. I have never seen one. The incident has been made prominent through the practice of line breeding, mostly in cutting horses. Line breeding is described as the mating of two individuals that are more closely related than the average of the breed. This is not to put line breeding down. One of line breeding's functions is to uncover genetic problems so that they can be culled from the population. Culling those affected prevents them from becoming parents. Properly used line breeding is an excellent breeding tool. If you are concerned about genetic purity and not passing harmful genes to future generations, do not purchase mares that are heterozygous for those conditions or breed them to stallions that carry these alleles.

All horse breeds have genetic defects and undesirable traits. As the largest breed association, the American Quarter Horse Association (AQHA) lists the following 7 genetic defects and undesirable traits in their handbook:

1. **Parrot Mouth**
2. **Cryptorchid**
3. **Hyperkalemic Periodic Paralysis (HYPP)**
4. **Polysaccharide Storage Myopathy (PSSM)**
5. **Glycogen Branching Enzyme Disease (GBED)**
6. **Hereditary Equine Regional Dermal Asthenia (HERDA)**
7. **Malignant Hyperthermia (MH)**

❷ *Thumb Rule:* **Don't purchase problems**

Excerpt from 2022 AQHA Official Handbook, Pages 59-62:

Genes come in pairs; each parent contributes one copy to the offspring. With respect to the autosomal dominant genetic diseases listed below (HYPP, PSSM, and MH), only one defective gene is necessary to express the genetic disease in question. Such gene can be inherited from either of the parents or from both of the parents. With respect to autosomal recessive genetic diseases listed below (GBED and HERDA), typically, two copies of an abnormal gene (two copies = a pair) must be present in order for the horse to show signs of the genetic defect in question. Horses with only one copy of the defective gene are considered "carriers".

Parrot Mouth - either overshot or undershot, defined by the American Association of Equine Practitioners as "no occlusal contact between the upper and lower central incisors."

Cryptorchid - meaning less than two visible testicles descended into the scrotum.

Hyperkalemic Periodic Paralysis (**HYPP**) - HYPP is an inherited autosomal dominant genetic disease. A muscular disease caused by a hereditary genetic defect that leads to uncontrolled muscle twitching or profound muscle weakness, and in severe cases, may lead to collapse and/or death. According to research, this condition exists in certain descendants of the stallion IMPRESSIVE.

Polysaccharide Storage Myopathy (**PSSM**) is an inherited autosomal dominant genetic disease that causes excess glycogen storage in muscles which can result in tying-up, muscle tremors, and/or gait abnormalities.

Reprinted with permission from the American Quarter Horse Association | https://aqha.com/aqha-rulebook

Glycogen Branching Enzyme Disease (GBED) is an inherited autosomal recessive disease that terminates protein synthesis which can result in late-term abortions or death in foals shortly after they are born.

Hereditary Equine Regional Dermal Asthenia (HERDA), also known as Hyperelastosis Cutis (HC), is an inherited autosomal recessive disease that weakens collagen fibers that connect the skin of a horse to the rest of the horse. Affected horses can have fragile hyperextensible skin which can result in tears, scars and lesions. Affected horses are also known to exhibit impaired healing to such injuries.

Malignant Hyperthermia (MH) is an inherited autosomal dominant disease that causes a life-threatening condition that is usually triggered by exposure to certain drugs used for general anesthesia. In susceptible horses, these drugs can induce an uncontrolled increase in skeletal muscle oxidative metabolism which affects the body's capacity to supply oxygen, remove carbon dioxide, and regulate body temperature, potentially leading to circulatory collapse and death if not treated quickly.

AQHA requires that both the stallion and mare have DNA on file with the AQHA before their offspring can be registered. All stallions must also have a Health Panel for the defects listed above on file (via DNA test) before their offspring can be registered – effective January 1, 2015. Foals conceived via fresh-cooled or frozen semen must have a DNA test to prove their parentage before they can be accepted for registration.

If needed, the foal owner pays AQHA the designated fee for the test, AQHA sends the foal owner a DNA test kit, the foal owner removes at least 50 hairs from the mane or tail by the roots and mails the DNA kit to the Equine Genetics Laboratory at the University of California, Davis. U.C. Davis completes the DNA test and sends the results to AQHA. AQHA then notifies the foal owner. AQHA becomes the sole owner of any and all DNA material and results. More information and order forms can be found here:

» *https://www.aqha.com/-/dna-and-parentage-verification*

Rusty and SAN SOMEBODY crossing the Maroon Creek headwaters, Colorado

FINAL THOUGHTS BEFORE PURCHASING

1. Do I really want to own a horse and devote most of my time outside of work to this activity? If the answer is yes, go to #2.

2. Have I really figured out the costs – both in time and finances?

3. Have I arranged a physical facility for keeping my horse?

4. Do I want this to be a hobby or a business?

Let's review the above questions:

1. Horse Ownership: This is pretty much self-explanatory. Assuming the answer is yes, we move to #2.

2a. Cost → Financial: The annual cost of keeping your horse can and will range widely from $2,000 to $10,000 per year.

2b. Cost → Time: This will be variable and will change from the short winter daylight hours to the longer summer hours. For maintenance duties only, you will need about 1 hour per day to feed and water twice a day and clean the stall or pen at least once a day. You'll also have some exercising and grooming to do. If you board at a full service facility they will do the above daily chores for you, at a cost, of course. Exercise and grooming may cost extra.

> ❷ *Thumb Rule:* **Time is also money**

3. Facility: The first-time horse owner should probably keep or board their horse at a full service facility. This should ensure that your horse is always being given the necessary attention. Initially, there are minor things that your horse needs that you may not be aware of, and only time and experience will make these items things that you don't have to think about but do intuitively.

Take care to know exactly what the boarding facility is responsible for. Responsibilities vary, but normal is pretty much daily feed (hay and grain), salt and mineral, water and stall cleaning. Blanketing, putting the horse on the walker, exercise and grooming are often extras because they take someone's time, and time is money.

Blanketing a horse requires 5-10 minutes to put on and remove. The same is true for putting the horse on and off the walker. Therefore, these two activities require 20-40 minutes daily. This is a daily cost of $5.00-$10.00 with $15/hr labor (25¢/minute).

Just be certain you know what is in your signed boarding contract. You also need to know how long the contract is for and how much advance notice you need to give should you decide to move your horse.

Most boarding facilities do not take responsibility for your horse's health and welfare other than what's discussed above. You are responsible for veterinary care, both routine and emergency. The boarding facility will need your Vet's name and phone number and have authorization to use its own Vet in case they cannot reach yours.

The boarding facility may agree to or want to be responsible for annual vaccinations and periodic deworming. You'll learn that you are responsible for the costs. You'll learn that you are responsible for many costs!

You are responsible for farrier work. Most facilities will have a farrier who makes regular visits. You may have them put your horse on their schedule or use your own farrier and do your own scheduling. Again, the cost is yours.

Insurance is often purchased for high-dollar horses. You can obtain insurance for every condition known unto horse but the cost goes up with the likelihood of occurrence of each condition insured. Most people only obtain a mortality policy, and many attach a colic surgery or major medical supplement. Mortality policies cost roughly 3-5% of the value of the horse.

A veterinary exam detailed by the insurance company is required up front, followed by annual exams. The boarding facility needs to be informed that your horse is insured, who the company is, and their phone numbers. This should be posted in a conspicuous place (on the stall) because it is necessary to call the insurance company should the horse become ill and need more than routine veterinary care. Call before treatment unless a dire emergency exists.

❷ *Thumb Rule:* **Be prepared**

4. Hobby or Business: Most first-time owners will probably consider their horse project a hobby for their personal pleasure. Some may actually plan a business from the onset. One needs to be aware of the Internal Revenue Service's (IRS) definitions of hobby and business. If you are planning a business, you should run your proposed business plan by a certified public accountant (CPA) who has experience with horse owners and their businesses.

As a business owner, you are able to charge expenses and depreciation against your income. You'll notice that there must be a plan in place to create income. The IRS has specific criteria that must be met in order for your horse interest to qualify as a legitimate business. If yours is to be a business, erase the word hobby from your vocabulary! More attention to a business program is given in part on page 126.

❷ *Thumb Rule:* **Hobby is no longer a horse word**

IRS: How do you distinguish between a business and a hobby?

» *https://www.irs.gov/newsroom/earning-side-income-is-it-a-hobby-or-a-business*

*"There's something about the outside of a horse
that is good for the inside of a man."*

—President Ronald Reagan

February 1977 – Former California Governor, Ronald Reagan, with his
Throughbred gelding, *LITTLE MAN*, at his Rancho Del Cielo in Santa Barbara
County, CA. An avid horseman, Reagan served as a reserve Cavalry Officer in the
1930s before becoming one of the most sought-after Hollywood cowboys.
As the 40th President of the United States, his passion for horseback riding
prompted the advent of the first Mounted Secret Service security detail.

Eddie Armstrong aboard a good Grade ranch gelding with his Mom, Linda, at the Willow Creek Ranch at the Hole-In-The-Wall in Kaycee, Wyoming

Part 3

NOW YOU OWN YOUR HORSE

Enjoy him! What a great situation. You've done all your homework, made prudent decisions and are now engaged in a future that knows no bounds. Congratulations!

You have your horse situated at a good boarding facility or on your own property. Your horse activity is firmly decided upon and established in your mind, and hopefully on paper.

For the horse in the wild – we still have Mustang bands in the western United States, and they exist in a survival of the fittest mode – the weak, the crippled and lame, the ill, those born conformationally inept and the slow generally do not live to be the progenitors of the next generation. Many of what we adopt from the Bureau of Land Management (BLM) today as wild horses would be correctly identified as feral horses – domesticated horses that have strayed away from ranchers or have been turned loose and have interbred with the wild populations. The Kiger Mustang herd in Oregon is a good example of true mustangs.

Having once been wild and now domesticated, horses still maintain their basic survival instinct of **flight or fight**. The last fifty years have experienced extreme selection in breeding horses for gentle dispositions. This is not true for the horses used for rodeo bucking stock. However, when severely pressured in scary situations, our horse can still exhibit flight or fight.

2023 U.S. BLM Wild Horse Population Estimate from 10 Western States = 68,928

Source: https://www.blm.gov/programs/wild-horse-and-burro/about-the-program/program-data (8/2023)

Many, or most, horses today appear to enjoy relationships with their owners and look forward to being petted, loved and ridden.

There are a few signs that your horse will exhibit when he is in a bad mood. The first is that he may pin his ears back and drop his head and neck. He may increase his bad mood by opening his mouth and charging with his ears pinned back; he may even turn around quickly with the intention to kick. This happens infrequently with humans, but horses often fight each other in this manner.

Photo ©Terri Cage (left) & Yurkovska Tanya/AdobeStock

The eyes have a habit of telling everything! They are great indicators of the horse's feelings. Should your horse be acting unruly as described above, take a whip or lead rope and spank him. The spanking must occur at the time the unruliness is happening. You must remember to keep yourself in a safe spot away from the horse. Yell at him to stop and whip his chest and front legs. Should he wheel around, whip his backend. Never whip or hit your horse in the head, as you could accidentally damage his eye.

You need to react quickly, pretty hard and then quit. If he lets you, pet him and tell him everything is okay. Stay aware of his eyes, head and body language. Most horses will never require this unless you have failed to discipline them for the small things and their behavior has gotten out of hand. A lot like a teenager!

❷ Thumb Rule: Always be kind to your horse but always discipline him for disobedience – never punish

SAFETY

Most horses are capable of being frightened and reacting quickly without regard to their handler. Because horses are large, athletic and sometimes unpredictable, it is important to know how to position yourself in order to prevent injury. The closer you stand to the horse, the less likely you are to be hurt. It is better for the horse to push you while you are close to him than to run over and knock you down when you are not close to him.

The horse has limited vision or blind spots in certain areas. We are all easily frightened when it is difficult to see clearly.

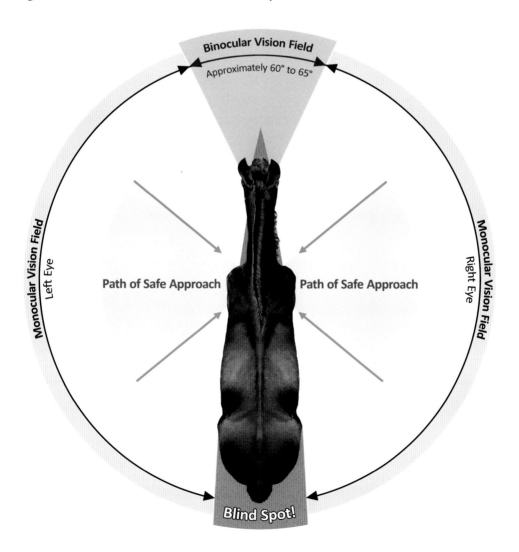

CATCHING & HALTERING

① Approach the horse at his left shoulder where he can clearly see you and place your hand on his shoulder. With the halter in your left hand, place the end of the lead rope over the neck with your right hand, grabbing it below with your left hand to temporarily prevent him from walking away. ② Reach your right arm over the neck and ③ grasp the crownpiece of the halter from your left hand from below the jaw. ④ Slide the noseband up over his nose with your left hand, then ⑤ pull the crownpiece up over the bridlepath behind the ears and ⑥ secure it to the cheekpiece.

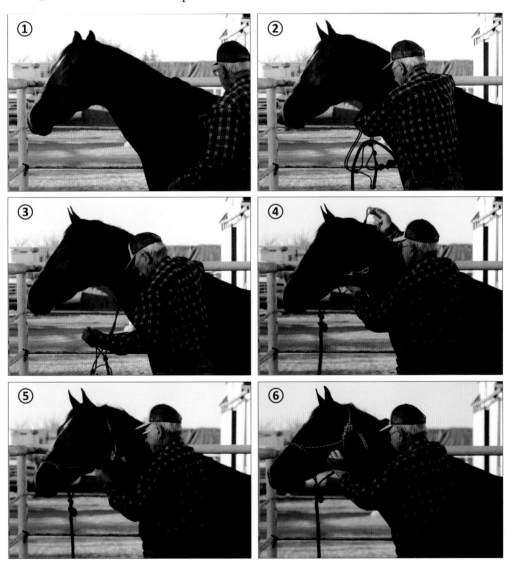

TYING A ROPE HALTER KNOT

Nylon halters with metal buckles are the most commonly used. But rope halters are a durable and affordable option, and you can easily make them yourself. For the unbroke horse, rope halters are less likely to break when the horse exerts extreme pressure on them. Tied incorrectly, the rope halter knot can be very difficult to untie under tension or in an emergency situation.

To tie the knot, begin by ① passing the crownpiece end underneath and out through the eyelet on the cheekpiece. ② Pass the end to the right, then underneath the eyelet – not over – pointing to the left. ③ Lastly, pass the end back to the right through the loop you've created and ④ pull it snug.

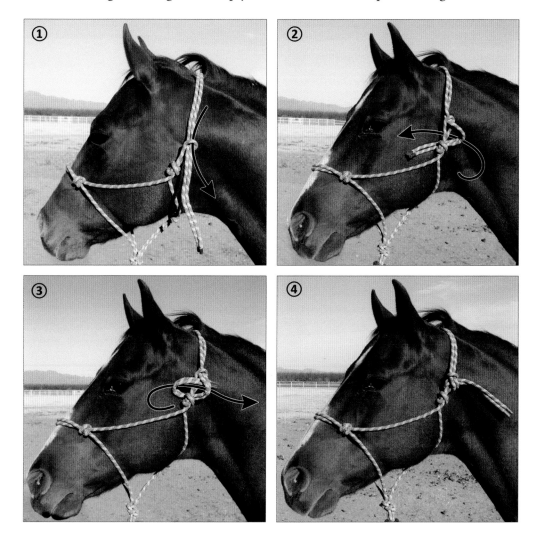

LEAD ROPES

A lead rope should not be more than 8 feet long. Most are 10-12 feet long which makes it easy for the lead rope to become wrapped around the handler's foot or leg. This is a serious (possibly deadly) accident looking for a place to happen!

HANDLING

When holding the haltered horse, we normally hold the lead rope in our right hand while standing on the left side of the horse, between the head and shoulder. The handler should stand reasonably close to the horse and have no more than 12-15 inches of lead rope between the handler's hand and the horse's halter. This enables the handler to react quickly to an unexpected motion by the horse.

Joe III showing METALLIC VON ROAN at Halter © Lori Gardner

This helps to prevent the handler from being run over and/or hit with the horse's head. The best way to control the frightened horse is to step back, pull his head toward you with the lead rope and make him go in a circle around you. Pulling the head to the side breaks the horse's forward motion and gives you the opportunity to regain control.

❷ *Thumb Rule:* **Never stand directly in front of a horse**

Josh & son, Eddie, preparing to show VON CHERRY at Halter at a La Mesa Open Horse Show

If another person is helping you with the horse, you should both be on the same side of the horse. This prevents the horse from hurting your helper when you turn him in a circle around you.

When leading the horse, stay on the left side and near the head so that the horse can see you. Horses should be taught to lead and turn from both sides. For whatever reason, we tend to do most of our handling and mounting of our horses from the left side. I am told it was because, years ago, swords were worn on the rider's left side, and mounting from the left side was easier. You and your horse should become ambidextrous in this regard. There are times during trail rides when the terrain will make it impossible to mount from the left without pulling your horse off the trail and down the slope.

> ✪ *Thumb Rule:* **The left side is the "Right" (correct) side**

WALKING BEHIND THE HORSE

When walking behind the horse keep your hand on the horse's hip, stay close to the horse and talk to him as you go around his backend (blind spot).

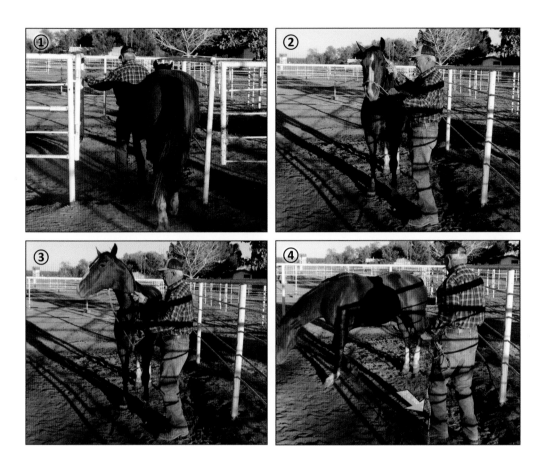

UNHALTERING & RELEASING

① When you take your horse into a pen or pasture to turn him loose, first turn him around 180° facing the gate through which you just brought him.
② Finish any petting you want to do while the halter is still on the horse.
③ Then remove the halter, and ④ step back and away from the horse. Some horses, when turned loose, will tend to run off and kick out (not for meanness but for the joy of freedom). By turning 180° and stepping back, you prevent being kicked, whether accidentally or on purpose, as the horse runs off.

You should leave the lead rope around the horse's neck for a few seconds to prevent him from getting into the habit of bolting and running away. You can get injured when they unexpectedly bolt and race away. Do not leave the halter on your horse when you turn him loose in the pasture or pen unless it is designed to break-away (see page 64). The horse may get the halter hung on something or get a foot through it and cause serious injury or death.

KNOTS & HITCHES

There are many knots, but most horsemen need to know only 3 or 4. Again, use a soft braided ¾ or 1 inch thick lead rope no more than 8 feet long.

1. Hitching Rail – The most common knot is a slip knot, and it is generally easy to tie and untie. Any knot can be very difficult to untie if the horse sets back and tightens it. One way to help prevent this is to ① wrap the lead rope two full turns around the hitching rail before tying the knot. If the horse sets back, the second wrap will prevent the knot from taking the full impact of the horse setting back.

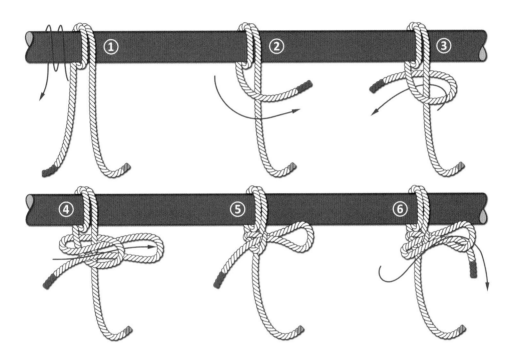

⑥ Always run the loose end of the rope through the bite-loop to prevent the horse from loosening the hitch with his teeth.

There should only be 12-15 inches between the hitch rail and the halter. Too long a tie could enable the horse to get a foot over the lead rope and cause a big wreck. Tie the horse 4-5 feet above the ground and be certain he is tied to something solid that will not break or come loose. It is a terrible sight to see a post or a fence board "chasing" a frightened horse!

2. Clove Hitch – A quick, useful knot, especially when tying to a round vertical post, pipe or object.

3. Bowline – An often-used knot because it will not slip and is relatively easy to untie. You will find many situations where the bowline is useful. It is difficult to tie a tight package or bundle with the bowline.

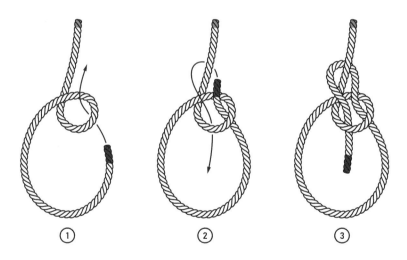

4. Square Knot – The basic of all knots. When tied properly, it holds strongly and is reasonably easy to untie.

Josh tightening a single-diamond hitch on a pack carried by COMO SE GUNNER on the trail with son Joe III & daughter Georgia in the Gila Wilderness, NM

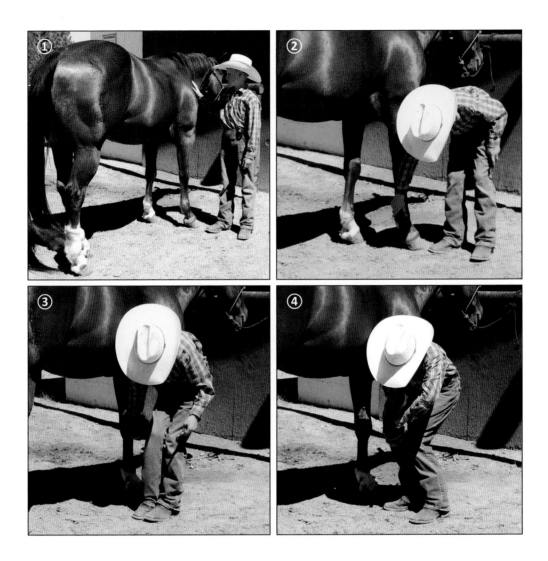

CLEANING THE FEET

It is important that you learn how to correctly pick up both the front and hind feet for cleaning, examination, trimming and shoeing.

The fronts are easier. ① Stand to the side of the front leg facing backwards; ② run your hand down the leg to the ankle (fetlock) and ③ lift the foot. Then it is best to ④ step across the foot and hold it between your legs for examination.

Hoof Pick

60

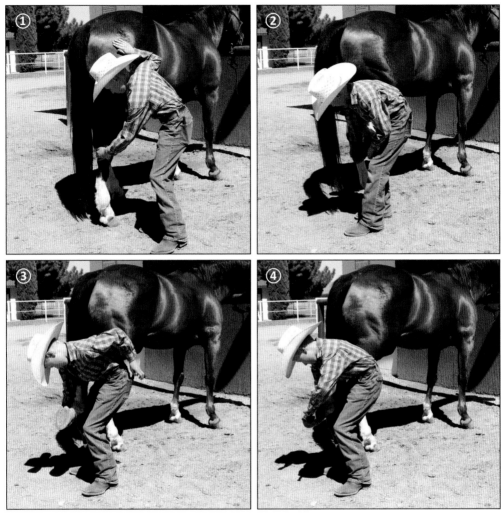

Eddie cleaning RANKINS REMINIC's feet

The hind or rear foot is more difficult and potentially dangerous. ① Stand beside the horse's hip facing backward with your inside hand (right hand if you're picking up the right hind foot) on the horse's right hip and run your left hand down the leg from the hock to the ankle. ② Pull the leg toward you, then ③ cradle it between your knees as you ④ step out to securely hold the foot for examination. Never just reach down and grab the hind foot. You might just get kicked or run over. The horse needs to see you and understand what is being done to him.

  ❷ *Thumb Rule:* **Remember – safety first, always!**

GENTLING YOUNG OR OLD HORSES

Ropes & Horses – It is important that your horse learn to respect and not be afraid of ropes. It is preferable to use a soft, larger diameter rope (¾ - 1 inch).

Begin by ① rubbing your horse with the lead rope. Put the rope over his back and on each side of his body. Be slow and easy to keep your horse from being afraid of the rope. Then lightly curl the rope around each front leg and then the hind legs. Just swing it gently and let it go around the leg. Be certain to maintain your proper position in relation to the horse in order that you may safely correct him should he want to run away from the rope.

Be gentle and quiet, but not timid. Let the horse know that the rope is a normal piece of equipment and will not hurt him. Once the horse accepts the rope around all legs, take the rope and teach him to let you ② pull each foot and leg forward. Don't hold for more than 2-3 seconds before releasing the foot to the ground. Release it gently; don't just drop it to the ground abruptly.

> ❷ *Thumb Rule:* **Never be timid & never be too aggressive**

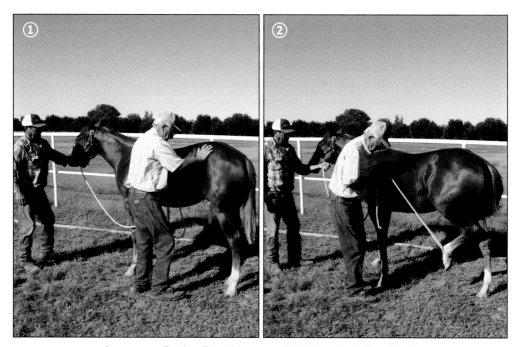

*Armstrong Equine Barn Manager Fidel Herrera & the author
using a lead rope to gentle yearling filly VON SUGAR LADY*

As the horse becomes used to his foot being pulled forward and is not afraid, you may increase the period of time that you hold it up. You should never need to hold it for more than 10-15 seconds.

This is also a good practice for helping to teach the horse not to panic, run away and hurt himself should his foot become caught in a fence, etc. It may not always work, but it is a good lesson to learn. It also makes hobbling easier should you decide or need to use hobbles on your horse (see page 68).

Be somewhat cautiously aggressive. Being timid can get you run over and hurt. Being overly aggressive can do the same, and both are harmful for the horse. You must be your horse's leader, not his follower. Every ship needs a Captain!

Maintain discipline and thereby command respect. Your demeanor of confidence should result in your horse being respectful of you.

> ❷ *Thumb Rule:* **The horse cannot be the boss!**

RESTRAINT

There will be times when restraint of your horse is an absolute necessity. Your horse may be injured, need medication, shoeing, or he simply will not behave. Remember, your safety is the main concern.

There are several methods of restraining the horse, depending on what needs to be done and the level of restraint the horse needs. This will make you appreciate proper discipline and training as the horse has grown up! Discipline is not bad or harmful. It is necessary.

Remember, the horse weighs 5 to 12 times more than his owner or handler!

> ❷ *Thumb Rule:* **Discipline & punishment are 2 different things**

Restraint methods include **voice and hand reprimands, twitches, tranquilizers** and **ropes**. Always use the minimal restraint for the problem but enough to accomplish the task safely (for both you and the horse).

A lead rope that has a chain on the horse-end is also a method to restrain the horse. For minor restraint, the chain goes over the nose. The chain can be put through the horse's mouth if more restraint is needed. Refer back to ground safety around horses on page 54 for human positioning during restraint.

Chain Over The Nose

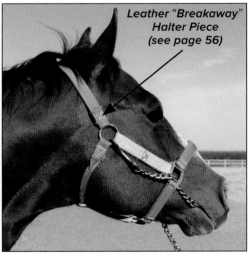

Leather "Breakaway" Halter Piece (see page 56)

Chain Through The Mouth

TWITCHES

The **twitch** is used on the nose and generally causes the horse to be more concerned with his nose than with what you are doing elsewhere. Most horses are respectful of the twitch but may give quite a bit of resistance to your applying it.

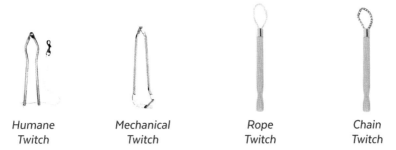

Humane Twitch   Mechanical Twitch   Rope Twitch   Chain Twitch

Never twitch the horse's ear. Be certain to stand beside your horse's head so that your heads are less likely to come into contact with each other's. You will lose! Always stand beside your horse when checking issues – never in front – and always keep your free hand on the horse's body in order to feel and anticipate his movements. This also lets the horse know where you are. It is best to stand close, even against the horse's shoulder, so that he pushes rather than runs into you should he become excited and choose to flee or fight. This procedure is good to use at all times, whether just observing, grooming, or treating your horse. Safety First!

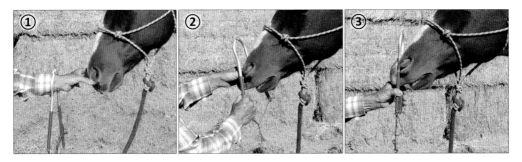

Always hold onto the twitch. If the horse gets away from you or throws his head, the twitch can become a dangerous object – much like a policeman's billy club! You can be seriously injured by the twitch.

Twitches are only to be used on the nose. Never twitch a horse's ear because you always approach this area whenever you halter or bridle your horse.

❷ *Thumb Rule:* **Never twitch the ear**

You may use your hand when only moderate restraint is needed: ① on the nose, or ② by taking a handful of skin on the neck. It simply shifts the attention from whatever he needs the restraint for back to you. When the twitch is removed, animal behaviorists advise to gently rub the nose (or neck) in a soothing manner. Horse psychologists say that the horse will remember this rather than the twitching. I recommend it and do it to my horses.

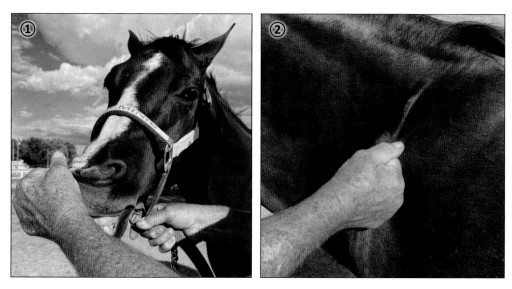

Tranquilizers – should only be used on the recommendation of your Vet. There are intravenous, intramuscular and either/or tranquilizers, and you can create huge problems and even death if they are misused.

Tying Up a Front Leg – a strap or soft rope can be used for restraining a front leg.

Tying Up a Hind Leg – a soft rope can be used to secure and restrain a hind leg. <u>This frightens most young horses</u> and must be done responsibly and correctly. Improperly done, this can hyperextend the horse's hock and stifle. If needed, use extreme caution and expert assistance. Follow the pictures closely.

This is an excellent time for a reminder that the handler and person tying the foot up should be on the same side of the horse to prevent one, the other, or both from getting run over should the horse get excited and try to run away.

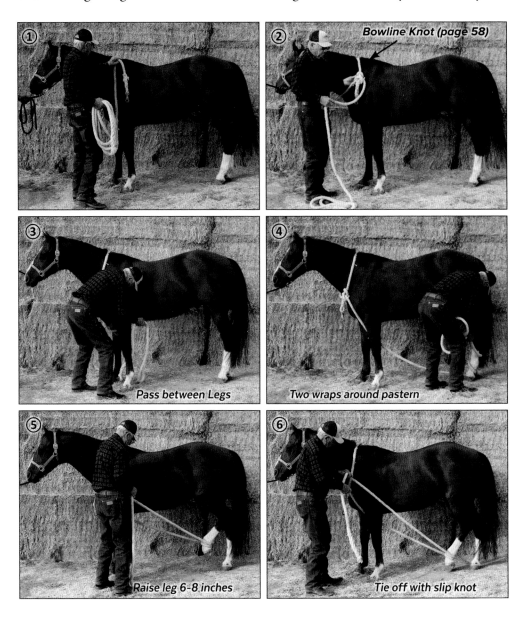

1️⃣

2️⃣ Bowline Knot (page 58)

3️⃣ Pass between Legs

4️⃣ Two wraps around pastern

5️⃣ Raise leg 6-8 inches

6️⃣ Tie off with slip knot

Hobbles – only if the horse is accustomed to them. I like to introduce hobbles to all horses. Not only does it help to keep them in a small area for grazing, etc., but they also teach the horse not to be afraid of ropes around the legs, which may keep them from serious injury if they ever step their foot over a wire.

Most hobbles are made of leather or a combination of leather and chain (see page 117). However, you can make your own hobbles out of a rope or even use your lead rope, as pictured to the right.

RANKINS REMINIC hobbled to allow a rest stop on a trail ride in the Gila Wilderness

The **War Bridle** (generally made of a nylon lariat rope) is another method of restraint and training. Used correctly, it is a good tool; used incorrectly, it is very dangerous to the horse's head and face. **Never tie a horse with a war bridle rope!**

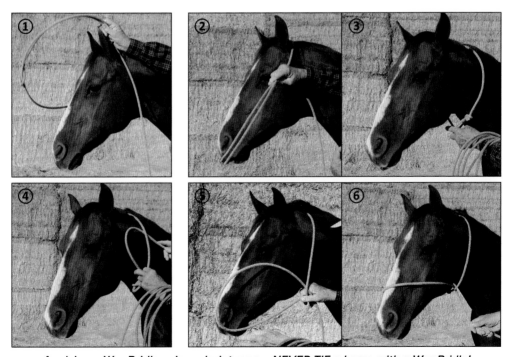

Applying a War Bridle using a lariat rope – NEVER TIE a horse with a War Bridle!

A **Chifney Bit** is often used when showing young horses at sales. The bit attaches to the halter and goes through the horse's mouth. It is similar to a bit. When used correctly it is an excellent mouthpiece for restraint. It gives you increased control.

Originally designed for Thoroughbreds, the Chifney Bit is now used on all breeds.

Chifney Bit snapped to sides of halter & attached to lead chain

Chutes – many people are injured every year, some seriously, by horses needing or being restrained. The horse's head, hooves and body weight are much harder and heavier than the handler's. The horse will win when not properly restrained. You are not being mean when you use proper restraint on your horse. It is for his and your benefit. Use of adequate restraint when needed generally results in your horse needing less restraint in the future.

> ❷ *Thumb Rule:* **The horse will win in a tug-of-war**

Utilizing a Squeeze Chute minimizes the possibility of sustaining injury to the horse or handlers

NEEDS

So then, what does your horse need? Before expanding the needs list, it is important to acknowledge that the horse's owner must realize that the horse's needs and the owner's wants are not necessarily one and the same! That being said, there is nothing wrong with the owner receiving satisfaction from knowing they are providing all and more than the horse needs. This is a part of the joy of ownership and should not be discouraged as long as the owner is financially able to afford the extras. However, these extras should never be added if they are a detriment to the owner's family and/or financial obligations.

Here is a list of needs and other items that will be discussed:

As we discuss needs, we are going to assume that we are dealing with a 1,200 pound (12 cwt.) mature horse. Smaller horses will require less of some things, and larger horses will require more. We will also assume this horse is used for moderate work. **Moderate work** is general riding for 2-3 hours per day.

Exercise Category	Heart Rate (BPM)	Example Activity
Light Work	80	Recreational Riding
Moderate Work	90	Training, Showing, Trail
Heavy Work	110	Ranch Work, Rodeo, Polo
Very Heavy Work	110-150	Racing, Eventing, Endurance

Source: National Research Council. 2007. Nutrient Requirements of Horses: 6th Edition. The National Academies Press. https://nrc88.nas.edu/nrh (8/2023)

We need to differentiate between **animal welfare** and **animal rights**. It is my belief that we are Biblically and morally obligated to take care of (provide welfare for) our horses. It is also my belief that the horse does not have the right to bite, paw, kick or run over me.

Today, most horses are kept in rather small, confined areas. This is unfortunate, but at least it gives most everyone the opportunity to own and enjoy a horse. Pasture is always preferred but is not an absolute need. Confinement necessitates forced exercise for the horse.

Forced Exercise on a Horse Walker

Line-Driving for Exercise or Training

NUTRITION

WATER

Water is the first nutrient needed by the horse. Water should always be available to horses – clean and free choice. The only time to withhold water is when the horse is extremely hot from being ridden hard. The hot horse should be walked to cool down and given small drinks of water until he is cooled down. Then he can be given free access to water.

The average horse at maintenance (doing no work) requires about ½ gallon of water per cwt. (100 pounds of body weight) per day. This means our 1,200 pound horse will drink 6 gallons of water at maintenance per day and may drink 10–12 gallons when worked hard, and, if the weather is extremely hot, up to 100 pounds of water (12 gallons @ 8.35 lb/gal)!

Water can be furnished via automatic waterers or by a hose and bucket. Automatic waterers ensure that water is always available (when they are working correctly). However, they should be cleaned often as the horse tends to slobber waste feeds in the water and/or will occasionally dump a load of feces (manure) in the water bowl. If the water bowl is on the back wall of the stall, you may look in and see water, but the horse may not be drinking because the water is putrid. Also, automatic waterers may break, spring leaks and freeze, but they are very convenient.

The advantage of watering with a hose and bucket is that you know how much the horse is drinking and that the water is clean. Often times, a horse will quit or decrease his drinking when he is getting sick. Watering with the hose gives you two to three minutes to observe the horse's physical condition, his stall for nails or damaged boards, the amount he has drunk, the feed he has or has not eaten, the condition and smell of his feces – his general health and well-being.

The disadvantages of watering with a hose are time and regularity. However, many people find this time very rewarding – just to study their horse and to slow themselves down.

The author giving PISTOLERO GAL a drink in Snowmass Lake, Colorado — Elevation 10,980 ft

FOOD

We generally think of hay and grains when we are feeding the confined horse.

Hay is also called roughage. There are many different kinds of hay that are acceptable for horses. Quality is the main attribute we look for. Quality means that the hay was cut at the optimal growth stage for maximum nutrient capacity, that it was baled at the proper moisture level and that the hay was clean of dirt and free of weeds and insects. Quality is expensive, but it pays for itself. You will have fewer veterinary visits and bills when feeding quality hay in adequate amounts to your horse.

FORAGE YIELD RELATIVE TO QUALITY AT DIFFERENT STAGES OF GROWTH:

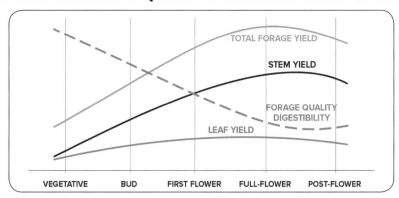

Adapted from Lacefield, G. Harvesting Alfalfa for Quality. University of Kentucky https://uknowledge.uky.edu/cgi/viewcontent.cgi?article=1337&context=ky_alfalfa (8/2023)

2% Cwt. Per Day – the amount of hay needed by the horse is approximately 2 pounds of hay per cwt. of horse per day:

2 lbs x 12 cwt = 24 lbs of Hay Per Day

(1,200 lb horse ÷ 100 = 12 cwt)

Quality hay will generally have about 6% moisture, so the 24 lbs x 94% dry matter provides your horse with 23 lbs of dry matter for his daily intake. This amount of high quality hay is all the nutrition many horses at moderate work require. If your horse loses weight, he should be given grain (discussed next) to keep his weight and activity level up. "The eye of the master fattens the horse."

❷ *Thumb Rule:* "Proper Feeding" always assumes adequate quantities of high quality feedstuffs

If you buy your own hay, you'll need about 4 tons (8,000 lbs) for each horse for a year. This assumes the horse does not have access to pasture. If you have room to store it, try to buy your hay by the ton weighed on correct scales. Buy first class hay, during the growing season. When buying by the bale be aware that hay bales come in differing weights. Some general weights are:

2 STRING BALES – ONE TON	**3 STRING BALES – ONE TON**
Average 67 lbs* or 30 Bales/Ton	Average 110 lbs* or 18.2 Bales/Ton
Approximate Size:	Approximate Size:
18″ wide x 36″ long x 14″ tall	22″ wide x 44″ long x 18″ tall
(*Bale weights can range from 40-75 lbs)	(*Indiv. bale weights can vary by 10%)

When purchasing hay in large quantities, try to store it off the ground (on pallets) and keep it under a shed or covered with tarpaulin.

Many people feed less hay and more grain. This will keep your horse fatter, but it may not be in his best interest. Excessive weight in horses, as in humans, places joints and general health under unnecessary stress. In the U.S., there are more overweight horses in confinement than underweight horses. The ideally conditioned horse is one whose ribs you don't see but can feel with your fingers.

The two basic kinds of hay are **legumes** and **grasses**. Legumes come from plants that fix nitrogen in the soil and generally have more protein and energy than grasses.

Alfalfa and **clovers** are the primary legume hays fed to horses. Alfalfa hays range from 14-22% crude protein (CP), and the mature horse only requires 8% crude protein. The excess protein from the alfalfa hay is used first for additional energy for your horse and secondly to provide fat stores.

The main disadvantage of alfalfa, assuming it is available at a reasonable price, is that it contains 6 parts Calcium (Ca) to 1 part Phosphorus (P). For the mature horse, this does not present a problem since he can metabolize an 8:1 Ca:P ratio. For young horses and broodmares, the ratio should be no more than 2:1 Ca:P.

Alfalfa   White Clover   Subterranean Clover   Sericea Lespedeza   Crimson Clover   Birdsfoot Trefoil   Red Clover   Common Vetch

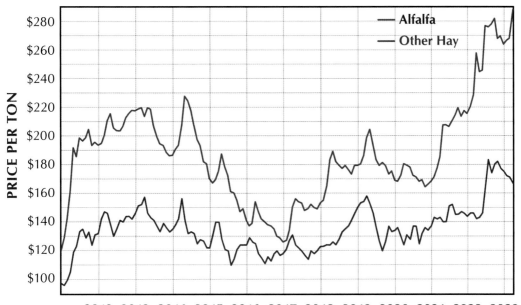

AVERAGE MONTHLY U.S. HAY PRICES (USDA-NASS)

Adapted from Hay & Forage Grower | Source: https://hayandforage.com (8/2023)

Therefore, it is recommended that a **12:12 mineral block** (or loose mineral) be available free choice when feeding alfalfa. The 12:12 mineral block contains 12% Ca, 12% P and 5% salt; the remainder is inert ingredients. No other salt should be available when feeding alfalfa and the 12:12 block. The horse eats the block to get the salt, and this forces him to get the required Ca and P. This ratio works for most horses.

12:12 Mineral Block

Grass hays are excellent, and many horsemen prefer them to alfalfa. A mixture of grasses and alfalfa is the best of both worlds. Grass hays fed to horses are **Bermudas, Orchard, Brome, Native, and Fescues**. There are others, but these are the most widely used.

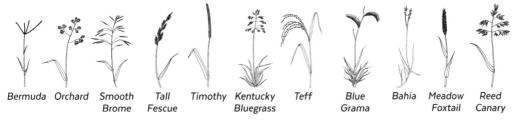

Bermuda Orchard Smooth   Tall   Timothy Kentucky   Teff   Blue   Bahia Meadow   Reed
                  Brome   Fescue   Bluegrass   Grama   Foxtail Canary

The nutrient quality of grass hay is often more variable due to stages of growth and cutting. Excellent grass hay will have 9-13% crude protein. Ca:P ratios are closer to the desired 2:1 ratio with grass hays. It is still a good idea to use the 12:12 mineral block as the only mineral available to your horse.

The 2% per cwt. per day is still a good rule for feeding grass hay. Some horses at moderate work will require additional grain when fed grass hays.

I prefer feeding hay free choice. I want the horse to always have hay when he wants it. I also prefer to feed at ground level. This is the manner in which a horse grazes, and it prevents dust and spores from being inhaled when he has to reach up to eat hay from a rack. If fed on the ground, some hay must always be available to prevent the horse from ingesting (eating) sand and possibly having sand colic. When hay is fed on the ground, it should be fed in a trough or large container.

Quality and quantity are more important than the kind of hay.

U.S. Dept. of Agriculture Hay Quality Designations:	% Crude Protein (CP)	
	Alfalfa	Grass Hay
SUPREME: Very early maturity, pre bloom, soft fine stemmed, extra leafy. Factors indicative of very high nutritive content. Hay is excellent color & free of damage.	> 22	N/A
PREMIUM: Early maturity, i.e., pre-bloom in legumes & pre-head in grass hays, extra leafy & fine stemmed-factors indicative of a high nutritive content. Hay is green & free of damage.	20-22	> 13
GOOD: Early to average maturity, i.e., early to mid-bloom in legumes & early head in grass hays, leafy, fine to medium stems & free of damage other than slight discoloration.	18-20	9-13
FAIR: Late maturity, i.e., mid to late-bloom in legumes, head-in grass hays, moderate or below leaf content, & generally coarse stemmed. Hay may show light damage.	16-18	5-9
UTILITY: Hay in very late maturity, such as mature seed pods in legumes or mature head in grass hays, coarse stemmed. This category could include hay discounted due to excessive damage & heavy weed content or mold. Defects will be identified in market reports when using this category.	< 16	< 5

Values based on 100% Dry Matter
Source: https://www.ams.usda.gov/sites/default/files/media/HayQualityGuidelines.pdf (8/2023)

Cereal Grains – oats, corn, barley and **milo** are grains that are used to supply energy for the work our horses are asked to perform. Most horse owners buy and feed **sweet feeds**. Sweet feeds are complete mixtures of grain, protein, fat, salt, minerals and sweeteners such as molasses to make the mixture palatable and to bind the finer particles to the grains.

| Oats | Corn | Barley | Milo |

Every feed manufacturer makes numerous sweet feeds for different classes of horses. Most all are balanced rations based on good scientific research. Sweet feeds are convenient and easy to use, but cost considerably more than single grains.

Feed no more than 1 to 1 ½ pounds of sweet feed (or single grains) per hour of activity for the mature horse at moderate work. Note that this is per hour of activity and not per cwt of body weight. This means 3 to 4 ½ pounds for 3 hours of moderate work. More strenuous activity may require additional feeding. A horse will seldom need as much as 10 pounds of grain per day.

Single grains are quite satisfactory where you are feeding horses individually – one horse in one stall or pen – versus several horses at the same feed trough at the same time. Some horses are like some people: gluttonous. They will eat too much and too fast and will be predisposed to colic, founder and other digestive problems.

❖ *Thumb Rule:* **Feed a maximum of 1 to 1½ pounds of grain(s) per hour of activity**

Oat is generally the grain of choice for most horse people. Oats may be fed whole or crimped (rolled). Oats are considered the safest of the cereal grains. They are safer because they have the highest fiber content and lowest energy value of the common cereal grains.

Whole   Crimped

Nutrient Content of Oats*

DE Mcal/lb	CP%	Ca%	P%
1.30	11.80	0.08	0.34

Corn has a reputation for being a hot feed. It does have the highest energy value and lowest fiber content of the common cereal grains. The problem with feeding corn is that most people feed too much. Too much energy coupled with too little exercise is going to make your horse frisky. It's probably not the corn, but the excessive energy you've provided him.

Example: Most of us feed our grain ration – sweet feed or single grains – by volume and not by weight. Weight is highly important, and you need to know how much your scoop or coffee can weigh when filled with different feeds. A one quart container of oats weighs approximately 1 pound. The same quart container of corn weighs 1 ½ pounds.

Couple the weight difference with the added energy or caloric value that corn possesses over oats, and your one quart of corn has two times as much energy or calories as your one quart of oats. When feeding corn, you feed less!

Corn is always cheaper than oats, and fed individually and correctly, it is an excellent feed. If finances are not an issue, I would recommend you feed oats or sweet feed. Sweet feeds are closer to oats in energy value.

Volume to Weight Comparison of Whole Grains:

OATS
32 fl oz = 1 lb
at Standard 14%
Moisture Content

CORN
18.3 fl oz = 1 lb
at Standard 15.5%
Moisture Content

BARLEY
21.3 fl oz = 1 lb
at Standard 14.5%
Moisture Content

MILO (SORGHUM)
18.6 fl oz = 1 lb
at Standard 14%
Moisture Content

*Grain weight varies based on actual moisture content

Corn can be fed as a whole kernel, ground, or flaked. Processing only increases the digestibility of corn by 6-8%. Therefore, if it costs 10% more to buy processed corn, just feed whole kernels. Again, only feed corn to individual horses in separate pens to prevent problems.

If steam flaked corn is fed, be certain that it contains no mold. In hot temperatures, the moisture can cause mold from steam flaking. This mold can easily cause illness and death. In very hot weather, feed whole kernel or ground corn. Throw any molded feeds away or return them to the feed store.

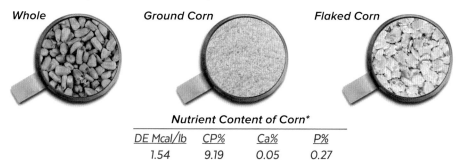

Whole   *Ground Corn*   *Flaked Corn*

Nutrient Content of Corn*

DE Mcal/lb	CP%	Ca%	P%
1.54	9.19	0.05	0.27

Barley is in between oats and corn as a safe feed and is a good source of energy. Barley is not grown in as many locations as are oats and corn. Barley seeds are harder than oats. Therefore, it should be crimped or rolled for horse feed. Barley is often less palatable than oats and corn. Fed properly, barley is a good feed for horses and may be fed as a single grain.

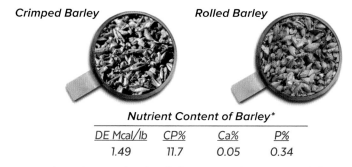

Crimped Barley   *Rolled Barley*

Nutrient Content of Barley*

DE Mcal/lb	CP%	Ca%	P%
1.49	11.7	0.05	0.34

Milo (grain sorghum) can also be fed as a single grain and has 90% the energy value of corn. Individual milo seeds are about the size of a BB and are very hard. Milo must be ground or rolled to make a good grain for horses. It takes most horses a week or so to begin to eat ground milo with relish. They will eat milo; you just have to start slowly and build them into it.

*As Fed Basis estimates of nutrient content for selected grains for reference only, actual values will vary
Source: National Research Council. 1989. Nutrient Requirements of Horses, 5th Revision Edition
https://nrc88.nas.edu/nrh*

If milo can be purchased for 15% less than corn, consider feeding it. I've fed corn or milo for years, and people always say our horses look great, have beautiful hair coats and want to know what kind of feeding program we use. I'm often hesitant to tell them for fear of bursting their bubbles!

Ground Milo   Rolled Milo

Nutrient Content of Sorghum (Milo)*

DE Mcal/lb	CP%	Ca%	P%
1.46	11.5	0.04	0.32

Sweet feeds usually cost two to four times the cost of corn per pound. Costs vary according to season, weather and supply. Again, if cost is no factor, use the convenience of sweet feed in a 40-50 pound paper bag. Be sure to price hays and grain products by the ton, not by the bale or bag. Do the math!

For performing horses, I recommend an 80:20 hay-to-grain ratio. 70:30 works for some people, but I prefer to err on the side of caution.

Today's sweet feeds generally contain 4% fat. This is good because fat increases energy content without increasing mass. Just like for you and me, fat contains 2.25 times as many calories as the same weight of carbohydrate (cereal grain). Liquid vegetable oil can also be added to the ration of horses that need more energy. Horses can handle 8% fat in their grain ration. Increasing the fat content means that you can feed less grain and still keep your horse in excellent condition. One cup of vegetable oil per day is a safe measure.

Complete, balanced rations can also be purchased as pellets, and hays can be purchased in cubes or wafers. These feed forms work well and may be easier to store.

For a new owner with only one or two horses, I recommend using a reputable feed manufacturer's balanced sweet feed

> ❷ *Thumb Rule:* **80% hay and 20% grain (max 30%)**

*As Fed Basis estimates of nutrient content for selected grains for reference only, actual values will vary National Research Council. 1989. Nutrient Requirements of Horses, 5th Rev. Ed. https://nrc88.nas.edu/nrh

SALT/MINERALS

It is best for the horse to have free access to a salt/mineral block. Again, 12:12 mineral is a good choice for most horses, and especially those fed alfalfa hay. It contains an adequate amount of salt, so no additional salt should be fed. Horses fed grass hay can utilize a normal salt block or mixture. Your horse will probably use one 50-pound block annually. Although some horses, like some people, will eat more. If the horse is salt deprived, when you give him his block his consumption may be great for a few days, but after a week or two, he will back off to normal consumption. You can also feed salt or minerals in granular form.

Horses licking a Salt Block

Photo ©Jirkaf/AdobeStock

ADDITIVES/SUPPLEMENTS

There are numerous additives on the market for every digestive, joint and arthritic problem known to horses. Many of these additives have little to no research behind their recommendations. Always ask for research results.

Your average mature, moderately worked, well conformed horse does not need these. Feeding a balanced ration of quality roughage and grains in adequate amounts will take care of almost all horses.

Young horses in hard training for cutting, cow horse, reining and roping may be candidates for supplements and joint injections. Ask your Vet and trainer. Again, if money is no issue and you'll sleep better at night, go for them.

If you also have cows, make certain that your horses have **No Access** to cattle mineral blocks that contain **Rumensin** (monensium sodium).

❷ *Thumb Rule:* **Rumensin is a killer for horses!**

Most horse owners will feed their horse(s) a commercially prepared grain ration plus hay. This is the best program if you only have one or two horses. There are many good horse feed manufacturers. Check with your consultant, trainer, or friends to determine the best feed source in your area for your kind of horse's performance.

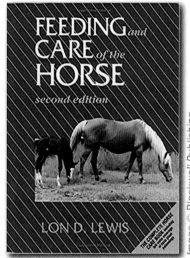

Image © Blackwell Publishing

My favorite resource text on feeds and feeding of horses is Lon D. Lewis' Feeding and Care of the Horse, 2nd Edition (Blackwell Publishing, 2005). I find this text to have a wonderful balance of the scientific and practical. Although it is a few years old, it answers 99.9% of my questions in a completely understandable manner.

CRITERIA FOR FEEDING:

- ☥ Fresh, clean water available at all times, except when a horse is hot and needs cooling down

- ☥ Feed high quality hay (roughage) at 2 pounds per hundred pounds of horse's body weight (cwt.)

- ☥ Feed grain as needed (3-5 pounds per day – fed ½ in AM and ½ in PM). Grain can be fed 3 to 4 times a day in smaller amounts

- ☥ Hay to Grain ratio: roughly 80% Hay to 20% Grain

- ☥ Salt/Mineral block or granular available, free choice

- ☥ Keep Stall/Pen clean of manure and trash

- ☥ Absolutely No Rumensin (monesium sodium)

- ☥ Supplements are generally not needed

Note:
- Cwt. (Centum Weight) refers to 100 pounds (Hundredweight)
- 1 U.S. Ton = 2,000 pounds (Metric Ton = 2,200 pounds)
- 1 kilogram = 2.2 pounds or 1 pound = 0.453592 kilograms

SHELTER

Shelter needs for your horse vary tremendously based on your geographic area. A covered box stall with an outside run is excellent when your horse does not have access to pasture.

Box Stalls with attached 18 ft x 36 ft Outside Runs

The standard box stall is 12 feet x 12 feet (144 sq.ft.). A 16' x 16' (256 sq.ft.) is more desirable, but again, cost becomes a factor, and most boarding facilities are constructed 12' x 12'. If you are dependent on a box stall arrangement, it would be great to have an outside run that is 12' x 24' or even 12' x 36' adjacent to the stall. The adjacent run allows you to leave the stall open and give your horse free run inside and out. You can also close the stall for cleaning or to just force the horse to be outside in fresh air and hopefully sunshine.

12 ft x 12 ft Box Stall

Fans help to keep fresh air moving inside barns and stalls

Ventilation is very important, even in cold climates. Stalls build up a reasonably high ammonia content from the horse's urine. It is important to keep the air your horse breathes fresh. The ammonia buildup is another reason for daily stall cleaning.

❷ *Thumb Rule:* **Ventilation is important to health**

Stall cleaning leads to bedding. In order to keep the horse from developing sores on the knees, hocks and pasterns from laying down on hard dirt and getting up, the stall will need to be bedded with shavings, straw or sand. Bedding can be as costly as the horse's daily feed ration.

Baled Straw

Bagged Sawdust Shavings

When housing your horse in a box stall, lights are a consideration. A horse that receives 16 hours of light a day (natural or artificial) thinks it is spring or summer. The light received via the eye affects the pineal gland. Horses shed their winter hair coat when spring or summer begins (as the days get longer and nights get shorter). Light, along with blankets, is our means of keeping the horse with short hair and in show condition all year.

If show condition is not desired, then forget the lights and let your horse grow his normal, protective hair coat. It will shed in spring as the days become longer. December 21 is the shortest day of the year, and June 21 is the longest. If you use the artificial light, it should be bright enough that you can read a newspaper anywhere in the stall or pen at night. A 100 to 200 watt bulb is generally sufficient for a 12' x 12' stall. Florescent light is also acceptable.

A simple time clock can be used and adjusted periodically to ensure the required 16 hours of light. I prefer to add the additional hours of light in the evening. It takes approximately ±60 days for the horse to become photosynthesized to the light regime. A flood light is effective in outdoor pens, provided it lights the entire pen.

❷ *Thumb Rule:* **Artificial light helps keep hair coats short in winter & also causes mares to become fertile earlier in the year**

100 Watt Stall Light with Bulb Guard   *Intermatic T100 24-Hour Mechanical Timer Switch with toggle switches for individual stalls on the left*

HEALTH CARE

Since we have domesticated the horse, he is now dependent on us for his health care. Wild horses ran on vast acreages, and often in dry country. Therefore, internal parasites were not a major problem, and survival of the fittest was also in play. Most horses today are kept in smallish confined areas, and internal parasites are a major problem.

Internal parasites are considered by many to be the major cause of death in the horse population today. The damage from internal parasites is a major cause of colic. This is a tragedy since prevention is so simple and effective, and the cost is negligible.

When you are considering purchasing a particular horse, you should ask for his health record to determine how often he has been dewormed, vaccinated (and against what) and what his illness history is. This information is not always available to you. Therefore, be certain you are dealing with a horse operation that enjoys a good, successful reputation. A pre-purchase exam by a good equine veterinarian is wise (see page 36).

INTERNAL PARASITES (DEWORMING)

Hopefully, the horse you purchased will have been on a good internal parasite prevention program his entire life, beginning at about 3 months of age and administered every 3 to 4 months thereafter.

Anthelmintic is the proper term for the compounds that we give our horses to prevent internal parasites. Our horses will never be 100% free of internal parasites, but we can effectively keep the numbers low enough that they do not cause significant damage. Plan to administer an anthelmintic a minimum of every four months. Every two months is more desirable in wet, humid environments.

Paste Anthelmintic syringe with adjustable dosages in 250 lb. increments

Paste Anthelmintics (dewormers) are acceptable, and you can administer them yourself. You set the gauge on the syringe to administer the proper dosage based on the body weight of your horse, remove the cap on the end, place it in the horse's mouth, and push the plunger. Be certain the anthelmintic stays in the mouth and is not spit out onto the ground. It is a good idea to hold the mouth elevated for 30 seconds or so to ensure the horse swallows or keeps the anthelmintic in the mouth.

Administering a dose of paste dewormer

The internal parasites that we are most concerned with are **Ascarids** (round worms), **Strongyles** (blood worms), and **Gasterophilus** (bots). Some anthelmintics are specific for bots, others are not. The bot fly lays its little yellow eggs on your horse's legs, chin, etc. Some geographic areas may require deworming for **liver flukes**.

My general rule is to be certain and use an anthelmintic that is specific for bots in the fall and in the early spring. The other two to four times, you can basically use any other. The anthelmintic that is or contains a boticide is slightly more expensive and can be used for each deworming. Change anthlemintics (dewormers) every year or two. Use a different chemical in the anthelmintic. Read labels carefully and/or seek the advice of your equine veterinarian. Parasites build up resistance over time, and not all horses are infected equally. **Fecal tests** are good to determine exactly what internal parasites your horse(s) may need to be treated for.

Parasites expelled in manure after deworming:

Ascarid
Round Worm
(Parascaris equorum)

Strongyles
Blood Worm
(Strongylus vulgaris)

Gasterophilus
Bot Fly Larvae
(G. intestinalis)

Parasite Life Cycle: Bot Fly (Gasterophilus intestinalis)

Adult bot flies quickly find a mate after emerging in the summer or fall months from pupa that burrowed into soil & dried manure. The adult female's lifespan lasts 7-10 days.

The female bot fly oviposits between 150–1,000 eggs onto the hairs of the horse. The eggs hatch into maggots (larvae) within 7–10 days of being laid.

Larvae are ingested or crawl into the horse's mouth & bury themselves in the gums, tongue or lining of the mouth, where they remain for approximately 28 days before moving into the stomach.

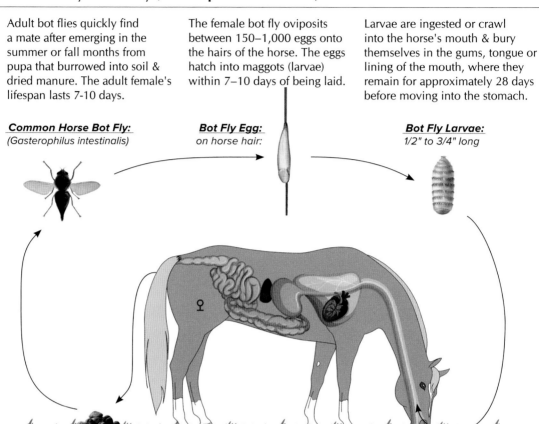

Common Horse Bot Fly:
(Gasterophilus intestinalis)

Bot Fly Egg:
on horse hair:

Bot Fly Larvae:
1/2" to 3/4" long

Once in the horse's stomach, the larvae attach themselves to the stomach lining, growing between 1/2 to 3/4 inches in length. After remaining immobile for 9-12 months, the larvae typically detach in late winter & early spring, passing from the horse's body in the feces where they pupate & remain for the next 1-2 months. The life cycle depends on the larvae overwintering in the stomach.

Indirect damage may occur from the annoyance of the hovering bot fly, causing the horse to stop grazing. Direct damages include severe irritation from the mouth infestation resulting in puss pockets, loosened teeth & loss of appetite; blockages leading to colic; tissue damage of the stomach & intestinal tract; & nutrients lost to the larvae's consumption. Other damages can include chronic gastritis, ulcers, esophageal paralysis, stomach rupture, squamous cell tumors & anemia.

Nine different species of Gasterophilus exist worldwide, with three commonly found in North America: G. intestinalis (gastrointestinal, shown above), G. nasalis (nose bot fly), & G. haemorrhoidalis (throat bot fly). Frequent grooming (bot egg removal) and deworming are recommended for the prevention of parasitic bots.

Ascarid, strongyle and other parasite life cycles are similar in that the horse ingests/inhales/absorbs the organism before eventually shedding the the eggs/larvae/worms in the feces, where the cycle repeats.

Reference:
Hiney K, Giedt EJ. 2017. Common Internal Parasites of the Horse. Oklahoma State University.
https://extension.okstate.edu/fact-sheets/common-internal-parasites-of-the-horse.html (8/2023)
McLendon M, Kaufman PE. 2019. Horse Bot Fly. University of Florida. entnemdept.ufl.edu/creatures/livestock/horse_bot_fly.htm (8/2023)

Weight tapes help you get an estimate of your horse's body weight (generally within ±10%). The weight tape derived value is acceptable for determining the amount of anthelmintic needed for your horse.

A more accurate weight estimation can be obtained using the **weight formula** published by Gibbs and Householder of Texas A&M. ① Measure the heart girth in inches (the circumference from the top of the withers around the belly, measured just behind the elbow) and ② length of the horse from the point of the shoulder to the point of the buttock (ischial tuberosity), then compute the weight using this formula:

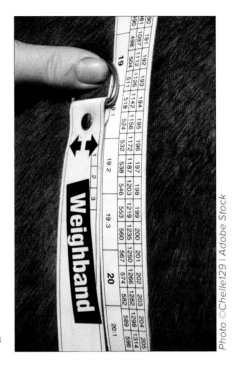

Photo ©Chelle129 | Adobe Stock

$$\text{(Heart Girth}^2 \text{ x Body Length)} \div 330 = \text{Pounds of Body Weight}$$

Source: https://animalscience.tamu.edu/equine-science-publications/ (8/2023)

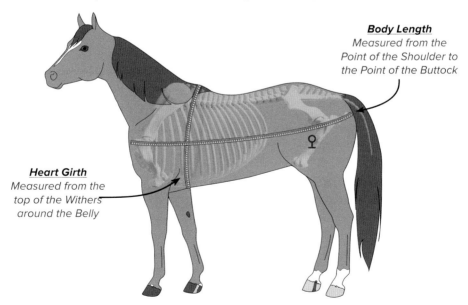

Body Length
Measured from the Point of the Shoulder to the Point of the Buttock

Heart Girth
Measured from the top of the Withers around the Belly

❷ *Thumb Rule:* **Use anthelmintics on schedule, based on your horse's weight**

VACCINES

The best approach is to first get the opinion of a good equine veterinarian in your area, preferably the one that will be your primary Vet. Certain areas will need more and different vaccinations than others.

Tetanus is the most necessary. The tetanus organism is responsible for the dreaded lockjaw malady. Both you and your horse should be vaccinated against tetanus. Fortunately, humans only need to be vaccinated every ten years. Your horse needs an annual vaccination.

The normal program is to use **tetanus toxoid** annually, which enables your horse to develop his own immunity to the tetanus organism should he come into contact with it. The first year, if your horse has not been on a tetanus vaccination program, you administer two tetanus toxoid vaccinations four to six weeks apart. Then your horse will only need one booster toxoid annually.

Tetanus Anti-Toxin is given to the horse that has been severely injured, cut, or has stepped on a nail. Tetanus anti-toxin gives immediate but short-term protection. If your horse has been on a good annual toxoid program, he may not need the anti-toxin when injured. Often the anti-toxin is given anyway for insurance, especially with severe lacerations or if you don't know what kind of vaccination program the horse has had.

Tetanus toxoid will do no good for the catastrophic injury situation because the horse requires too much time to develop its own protection.

❷ *Thumb Rule:* **Tetanus toxoid & tetanus anti-toxin are very different**

Eastern & Western Equine Encephalitis (**EEE** & **WEE**, also known as Sleeping Sickness), **West Nile Virus** and **Rabies** are the other vaccines that are generally considered standard, annual vaccinations. Although rabies is extremely rare, it is invariably fatal. While not considered core vaccinations by the American Association of Equine Practitioners (AAEP), **Influenza** and **Equine Viral Rhinopneumonitis** (**EHV**, also known as Equine Herpesvirus) are other vaccines that are often used on horses that travel to shows, etc. Consult your vet regarding risk-based threat concerns affecting your area.

RECOMMENDED SCHEDULE OF CORE VACCINATIONS FOR ADULT HORSES

Courtesy of the American Association of Equine Practitioners

ALL VACCINATION PROGRAMS SHOULD BE DEVELOPED IN CONSULTATION WITH A LICENSED VETERINARIAN

PREVIOUSLY VACCINATED	UNVACCINATED OR LACKING VACCINATION HISTORY
TETANUS **Recommendation: Annual**	**TETANUS** **Recommendation: 2 Doses** *Booster 4-6 Weeks after Primary Dose;* *Annual Revaccination*

Booster at time of penetrating injury, or prior to surgery, if last dose was administered more than 6 months previously

EEE/WEE **Recommendation: Annual** *Spring: Prior to the onset of Vector Season*	**EEE/WEE** **Recommendation: 2 Doses** *Booster 4-6 Weeks after Primary Dose;* *Revaccinate Prior to onset of next vector season*

Consider 6-month revaccination interval for horses less than 5 years of age and for horses residing in endemic areas and immunocompromised horses

WEST NILE **Recommendation: Annual** *Spring: Prior to the onset of Vector Season*	**WEST NILE** **Recommendation: 2 Doses** *Booster 4-6 Weeks after Primary Dose;* *Revaccinate Prior to onset of next vector season*

Consider 6-month revaccination interval for horses residing in endemic areas, juveniles (1-5 yrs old), geriatric horses (more than 15 yrs old) and immunocompromised horses

RABIES **Recommendation: Annual**	**RABIES** **Recommendation: 1 Dose** *Revaccinate Annually*

While the incidence of Rabies in horses is low, the disease is invariably fatal and has considerable public health significance. This is why it is a recommended core vaccine.

Read about AAEP suggested Risk-Based Vaccinations and Foal & Broodmare recommendations here:
https://aaep.org/guidelines/vaccination-guidelines

See current Risk-Based Threats & Locations monitored by Equine Disease Communication Center here:
https://equinediseasecc.org/alerts

Vaccination schedule developed by the AAEP Infectious Disease Committee, 2008 & updated by the AAEP Biological & Therapeutic Agents Committee in 2012 & again updated by AAEP Vaccination Guidelines Review Task Force in 2015.

Venezuelan Equine Encephalitis (VEE) is sometimes recommended. Unless your Vet says you should vaccinate for VEE due to an outbreak, I do not recommend it. According to the USDA, it has not occurred in the U.S. for over 40 years. In addition, your horse will show a **titer** (concentration of an antibody) in future blood tests, which could prevent you from being able to export your horse should such an opportunity arise.

The most recent reported case of a VEE outbreak was in October 2019 in Corozal, Belize, affecting five unvaccinated horses (*source: wahis.woah.org*).

❷ *Thumb Rule:* **Stay current with your Vet on new diseases & vaccines**

Eastern Equine Encephalitis in U.S. Horses 2001–2021 (USDA)

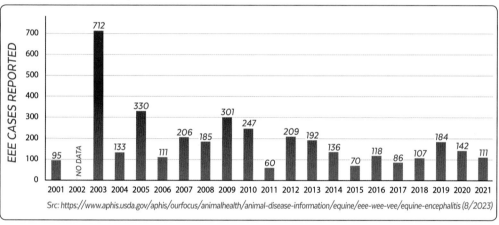

Src: https://www.aphis.usda.gov/aphis/ourfocus/animalhealth/animal-disease-information/equine/eee-wee-vee/equine-encephalitis (8/2023)

West Nile Virus in U.S. Horses 2001–2021 (USDA)

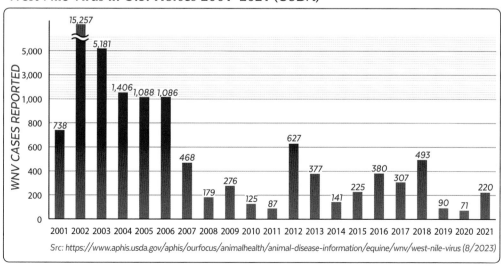

Src: https://www.aphis.usda.gov/aphis/ourfocus/animalhealth/animal-disease-information/equine/wnv/west-nile-virus (8/2023)

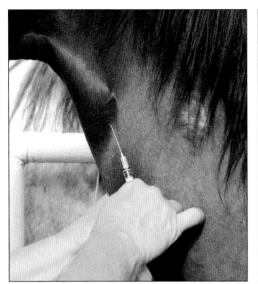 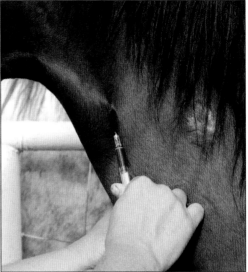

Veterinarian drawing blood intravenously from the jugular vein for a Coggins test

COGGINS TEST

The Coggins test is not a vaccination but a blood test that indicates the presence (positive) or absence (negative) of **Equine Infectious Anemia** (**EIA**, also known as Swamp Fever). The test is actually to denote whether the horse is a carrier for EIA. All positive horses die. Carriers can spread EIA. You should never purchase a horse without a negative Coggins test.

Coggins tests are generally good for twelve months, although some states require a negative test every six months.

Equine Infectious Anemia in U.S. Horses 2001–2021 (USDA)

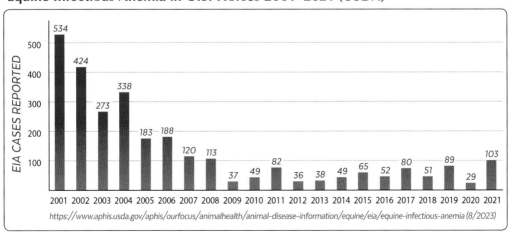

https://www.aphis.usda.gov/aphis/ourfocus/animalhealth/animal-disease-information/equine/eia/equine-infectious-anemia (8/2023)

TEETH

Teeth are important for proper harvesting and mastication of roughage and grains. The incisors should meet in order to easily harvest grasses. An overbite is known as **parrot mouthed**, and an underbite is called **monkey mouthed**. Both of these conditions are undesirable (see page 20). However, when a horse is provided his roughage in the form of hays and his grains are provided daily, most horses with mal-oclusive incisors are able to stay "fat and happy" and be successful athletes. In halter classes, stallions and mares (not geldings) with an over or under bite will be disqualified, depending on the Breed Association's rules. Over and under bites are considered to have a genetic tendency.

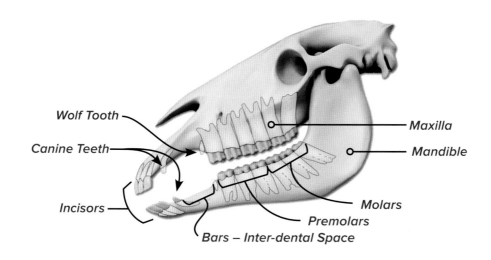

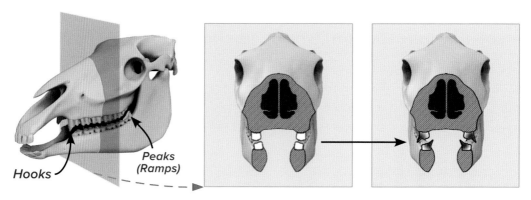

The teeth continue to erupt throughout the horse's life and are naturally ground down by mastication (chewing). As seen in the cross-section view above (center), the upper jaw (maxilla) is wider than the lower jaw (mandible) causing the molars to wear unevenly and form sharp enamel points.

*Technician floating a horse's teeth using a rotary power tool
with the aid of a ratcheting dental mouth speculum gag*

The horse's molars need to be observed periodically. The horse has a great capacity to grind feeds with his molars. The grinding is done with a somewhat sideways or elliptical motion. This motion can result in **hooks** and **peaks** on the inside and outside of the molars. The hooks and peaks can cut the cheeks and tongue and make the mouth so sore that the horse does not chew his feed adequately or even quits eating.

Years ago, most horses lived outside and roamed the range. They picked up rocks, sticks, etc., in the process of normal foraging, and this tended to keep the hooks and peaks at a minimum. Today, most horses only eat manufactured feeds that come from the feed store, thus necessitating regular dental check-ups.

When you notice your horse slobbering his feed and leaving excessive amounts in his water, he may need his teeth **floated**. Floating is the process of rasping off the hooks and peaks. Older horses may need their teeth floated annually. Some young horses will also need floating. Older horses often gain weight after

Photo Courtesy of the © Bryan College Station Eagle/Beverly Moseley

*Dr. Doug Householder inspecting a horse's mouth & teeth without a
mouth speculum, using a hankerchief to securely grip the tongue*

floating their teeth. Many performance horse trainers feel that the teeth should
be floated every 6-12 months in order to create more sensitivity to the bit when
being shown.

Care should be taken when feeling a horse's molars to see whether or not they
need floating. If a mechanical dental mouth speculum is not available and you
just place your hand in the mouth, you can be bitten harshly and have your
hand or fingers broken. You'll note that there is an interdental space between
the incisors and the molars that does not have teeth. This area is known as the
bars. Through this area, grasp the tongue and gently pull it out and up between
the molars. Do not pull hard. Now you can feel for hooks and peaks.

If the horse becomes upset, quickly remove your hand from the oral cavity and
release the tongue. Firmly holding onto the tongue while the horse moves its
head quickly can tear the tongue at its base.

❷ *Thumb Rule:* **Consider annual dental check-ups**

FARRIER

The farrier, or horseshoer, will be a major player in your horse ownership. Most mature horses need their feet trimmed every eight weeks. The same is true for shoeing – maybe even sooner. If your horse is ridden in sandy areas without rocks, he may not need to be shod unless his feet are brittle and break off easily. Most horses that are shown regularly will be kept shod. When the horse is not shown or ridden regularly for an extended period of time, it is good to remove his shoes and let him go barefoot. This gives the feet the opportunity for normal expansion and flexion.

Your farrier should be accessible, a good horseman and patient with horses. The farrier may have to discipline your horse at times (especially if you do not), but should not be angry or harsh with your horse. You may go through several farriers before you find one that fits you and your horse's temperament. Be fair and make sure you have your horse disciplined and obedient! Tranquilizers and/or twitches are sometimes needed (see page 64).

The author halfway through his half of one of the 250 head on the
Philmont Scout Ranch, Cimarron, New Mexico – 1956

FORCE = MASS X ACCELERATION

Our gelding bears his 1,200 lb. body weight on a combined surface area not much larger than the size of this page (4 hooves equal approximately 96 in^2, this page equals 70 in^2). On hard surfaces, the load bearing surface is further reduced to the outer hoof walls, or the surface area of the horseshoes – approximately 40 in^2 total!

At high rates of speed, the forces exerted on a horse's feet, legs and joints are immense. Researchers have measured the loading force on a running horse's feet at 2.5 times their body weight. The ground reaction force (equal in magnitude and opposite in direction) sends shockwaves vibrating up the leg at about 35 Hz with an impact speed of 5 meter/sec.

Considering the tremendous forces acting on the horse in motion, the paramount importance of proper conformation and a quality foundation is clear.

Impact Phase	*Midstance Phase*	*Breakover Phase*	*Swing Phase*
When the hoof initiates contact with the ground the total load is low, little more than the weight of the hoof	*At high speeds, the force can exceed 2.5 times the horse's weight (1,200lbs x 2.5)*	*The horse is propelled forward & the load decreases to equal the body weight*	*The hoof leaves the ground, accelerating to catch up with the horse*

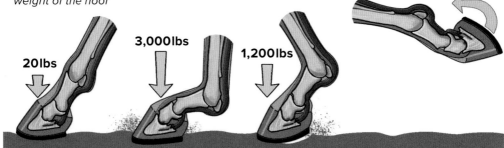

Source: Halucha D. 2019. Asymmetrical limb loading in Thoroughbred racehorses as a possible cause for injury. Univ. of Guelph. https://atrium.lib.uoguelph.ca/xmlui/bitstream/handle/10214/17263/Halucha_Danielle_201908_Msc.pdf (8/2023)
Peterson M. 2009. Measuring factors of a horse's gait in order to design safer tracks. University of Maine. (8/2023)
Illustration (adapted) courtesy of Racing Surfaces Testing Laboratory http://www.bioappeng.com /Horse/Public_mat.html (8/2023)

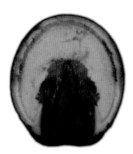  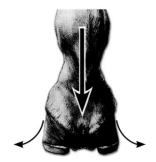

A properly shod hoof is symmetric – approxiamtely as wide as it is long	*Horseshoes are not nailed into the rear of the hoof to allow the heel to flex & expand under load*	*When compressed under load, the hoof wall & heel expand laterally to absorb the force of impact*

Farrier Clint Powell hot-shoeing VON NIGHT TRAIN's hind feet with sliding plates which help reining horses reduce friction when executing a sliding stop manuever

VITALS

First aid is needed for unexpected injuries and critical situations. Hopefully, most are minor, but they can be catastrophic. Knowing how to manage emergencies and staying calm are the two ingredients for success in first aid. Knowledge of the horse's vital signs is a must.

TEMPERATURE

Horses, like people, vary somewhat in their individual normals (99°F to 101°F). It is a good idea to establish a baseline for your horse. Veterinary thermometers are desired because they are sturdier and generally have a cord attached for easier control. A human thermometer can be lubed and inserted into the horse's rectum to obtain body temperature. It is important to hold and maintain contact with the thermometer while it is in the horse's rectum.

104°F (40.0°C) & greater is a **High Fever**
102°F (38.9°C) is considered a **Mild Fever**
100.5°F (38.0°C) = **Normal**

Increases in body temperature are indicative of infectious situations. Viruses are generally ushered in with a rapid high temperature: 104°-106°F (40.0°-41.1°C). Bacterial infections begin slower, although they too can become extremely high. Always take your horse's temperature before calling the Vet, and tell them what the temperature is. This will help your Vet know just how serious your situation is and how quickly they need to get to your place.

❷ *Thumb rule:* **Take horse's temperature before calling Vet**

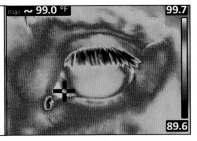

The use of non-contact infrared thermometers (NCIT) on horses has shown a correlation within 1°F (0.5°C) between the temperatures recorded with a digital rectal thermometer and the surface temperatures measured using a non-invasive NCIT near the eye (medial canthus).

Source: Carter, Dimitrova & Hall. 2019. Field testing two animal-specific non-contact thermometers on healthy horses. Veterinary Nursing Journal, 34:4, 96-101, DOI: 10.1080/17415349.2018.1559115. (8/2023)

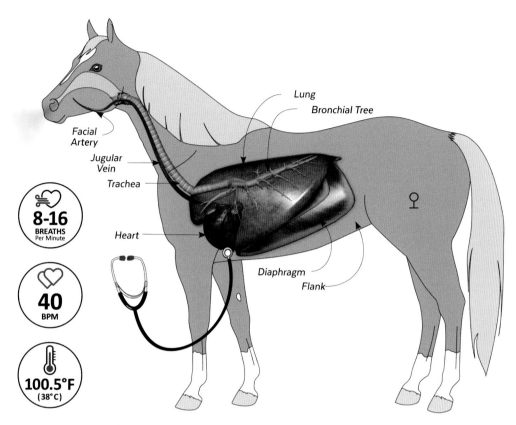

Facial
Artery

Jugular
Vein

Trachea

Lung
Bronchial Tree

Heart

Diaphragm
Flank

8-16
BREATHS
Per Minute

40
BPM

100.5°F
(38°C)

Average normal vital signs of horse at maintenance

RESPIRATION

Normal respiration is **8-16 breaths per minute**. During hotter, humid weather and/or after exercise, the respiration rate is naturally higher.

Respiration rate is observed by watching the rise and fall of the horse's flank or by observing the vapor from his nostrils in colder weather as he exhales.

HEART RATE

Normal is about **40 beats per minute** (BPM) at rest. Injury and infection elevate the heart rate. Heart rate can be measured with an inexpensive stethoscope or by pressing your finger over the facial artery just under the jaw and counting. Generally, you count the number of beats in 15 seconds and multiply by 4. If checking manually, do it at least twice before making your final determination.

HYDRATION

Capillary Refill is a good indicator of the horse's state of hydration. Simply pinch and pull the skin outward on the side of the neck, and see how long it takes it to return to normal. If it returns to normal in **5-10 seconds**, we assume the horse is adequately hydrated. A longer response indicates dehydration and is cause for concern. Let your Vet know.

You can also part the horse's lips and observe his gums. The color should be pinkish. If the color is bluish, you have a problem with circulation. Take your

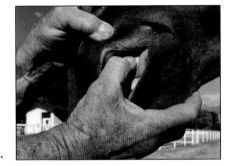

thumb or finger and press it into the gum, and observe how long it takes the tissue to return to normal. The color should return in 1-2 seconds. Observation of the gum color and refill is important in determining how severe the situation is. This is especially true in colic situations, discussed on the next page.

BLOOD

The average horse has 50-60 quarts of blood and can lose 10% before it is critical. Ten percent is 5 quarts, which is more than a gallon! So don't let the fact that your horse is bleeding from a cut or injury throw you into a panic.

If the blood is pulsating or spurting, an artery has been severed, which presents a more critical scenario than a slow stream of blood. Someone should apply compression to the arterial bleeding while someone else calls the Vet. Use clean bandages or clothing and enough pressure to stop the bleeding. Do not use a tourniquet unless compression is ineffective. If you do use a tourniquet, it should be loosened for 10-15 seconds every 3-5 minutes.

A humane twitch is not a vital sign, but it may be vitally important in helping you examine and treat your horse (see page 65).

> ❷ *Thumb Rule:* **Unless your horse is bleeding badly, first record temperature, respiration rate, heart rate & capillary refill before calling your Vet – relay these values as well as any symptoms or behavior you have observed**

TEMPERAMENT, LAMENESS & COLIC

We have already discussed most of a horse's physiological norms. The owner and barn manager must both do regular behavioral assessments of your horse in order to prevent him from becoming seriously ill. This topic is worthy of a book of its own, and all potential problems will not be discussed here.

It is assumed that you used solid advice from your confidants and purchased a good, sound, healthy horse. However, all horses are subject to developing health problems as they are used and as they age.

Noticeable changes from normal include depression, changes in temperature and pulse rate, changes in temperament and lameness. The key is to determine the causes of these changes. The horse's foot is the source of many changes. Lameness is the major problem and can have many causes, both simple and complex.

THRUSH

A degenerative condition of the frog caused primarily by failure to keep your stall clean and dry. There will be a black, foul smelling liquid that, once you get it on your hands, you will always remember it! Treatment involves cleanliness and proper medications, which are readily accessible. Left untreated, thrush can become severe and cause lameness.

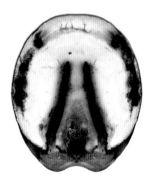

Black areas around the hoof wall & frog resulting from Thrush

❷ *Thumb Rule:* **Cleanliness is a virtue**

LAMINITIS OR FOUNDER

Laminitis first shows itself as pain in the feet. It can be in all four feet but is normally in the two front feet. In acute cases, the horse will tend to place his hind feet further up under his stomach and put more weight on the heels of his front feet. The Vet should be called immediately to begin treatment. Treatment aims to prevent the downward rotation of the coffin bone toward the hoof sole. The rotation occurs because the laminae that bond the coffin bone to the hoof wall have become inflamed and tend to release their contact with the coffin bone.

The primary cause or predisposing factor for laminitis in most riding horses is overeating grain. This may occur because the horse is simply fed too much grain or because he gets out and gets access to your grain supply. Laminitis can also occur from too much cold water when the horse is extremely hot. Trauma from being worked on too hard of a surface and some medications can also cause laminitis. Remember the 80:20 hay to grain ration.

NAVICULAR SYNDROME

Navicular appears to have a hereditary component. Horses with small feet and upright pasterns are candidates for navicular. The horse with navicular is normally a using age horse (4-18 years of age) that undergoes reasonably hard work such as roping, reining, etc. The horse with navicular will tend to intermittently stand with a front foot stretched forward the day after having been worked. The next day he may be sound, but hurting again the following day. Call your Vet and your farrier to develop a treatment program.

DISTEMPER OR STRANGLES

The bacterium *Streptococcus equi* is responsible for distemper. After a 3-8 day incubation period, there is fever, depression, a gross yellow puss, thick nasal discharge and swollen abscessed lymph nodes in the throat area. Breathing becomes difficult. The abscesses generally rupture in 10-14 days. They usually rupture to the outside but can rupture internally. The internal rupture can cause death or serious illness.

You will seldom see a more pathetic horse! They often stand by themselves with their head down to drain this gross discharge from the nose. Check with your Vet for their desired treatment plan. They vary considerably based on individual experience. My experience has been that if they do not stop eating and drinking, they will be okay in 2-4 weeks.

There are vaccines against distemper, and they seem to be becoming more proficient. Stalls and equipment used should be thoroughly disinfected. Stalls should not be reused for 4 weeks! Proper hygiene and cleanliness are a must. Once the organism is on a farm or ranch, it will spring up again. Often, the horse that has had distemper will seem to be immune (but not always).

COLIC

The short definition of colic is "pain in the gut". However, colic is the number one killer of horses. This is one of the reasons you have been encouraged to purchase your new horse from someone who has an excellent reputation for the health management of their horses. You were also encouraged to look at health records and veterinarian reports on the horse you have decided to purchase.

Damage done by internal parasites, beginning early in the horse's life, is the primary cause of colic. This is why the preventative measure has been to deworm all horses with a veterinary-specific anthelmintic 3 to 4 times annually, beginning at 3 to 4 months of age (page 88). This will not prevent colics, but it is essential to good health and a long life.

One of the more common causes of colic is your horse getting out of the stall at night and gorging on an open sack of sweet feed or cereal grains. Your stalls need good, secure latches. No midnight snacks!

Colic may also result from the horse being worked too hard, especially in extremely hot weather, being ridden on extremely hard surfaces, and by drinking too much cold water when he is extremely hot and tired. Give him small sips until he has cooled down and is quiet. Some medications can cause colic.

Colic's most visible sign is the horse picking at his stomach, rolling on the ground and sweating. All horses enjoy rolling in the sand, but this is more intentional and sometimes violent rolling. Time is of the essence when your horse colics. Call your Vet immediately, relay your horse's vitals, and tell them how he is acting. Ask what you should do for your horse while you await the Vet's arrival. Your Vet will probably want you to walk the horse in order to prevent violent rolling. If you have a stethoscope, listen to your horse's lower left stomach area for gut sounds. Gut sounds are positive. The absence of any sound makes the colic extremely serious and necessitates good vet care and advice.

The coliced horse can be very dangerous because of his pain. Use extreme caution not to be hurt by his hoof, head, or body. Be cautious. Most cases can be resolved with early veterinarian care. However, some are extremely difficult and may require surgery in order to save the horse's life. Surgery and recovery are extremely expensive. Unless the horse is insured for colic surgery, most people cannot afford the cost of the surgery. This makes prevention all the more important. All colics cannot be prevented by proper care and management. Sometimes it just happens.

> ❷ *Thumb Rule:* **Colic is the number one killer**

MUSCLE STRAINS & CHIROPRACTIC ISSUES
Just as with the human rider, horses can also develop strains and joint problems. Check with your Vet. There are many therapies and mechanical treatments available today. Acupuncture is also valid for certain conditions.

TRAVELING
When traveling to shows, rodeos, etc., don't use common watering troughs. If possible, water your horse with your own bucket. Safety first!

QUARANTINE
New horses arriving at your boarding facility should be placed in a quarantine stall away from other horses. Even though they arrive with a valid Health Certificate, they could still be incubating a problem that did not show up when the health paper was made. Quarantining for a three week period will give time for any disease the new horse may have been incubating to show up. It is not always possible to have a quarantine stall or area, but it is a good concept.

Common Conditions Affecting Horses Age 5 to Less Than 20 Years Old (USDA)

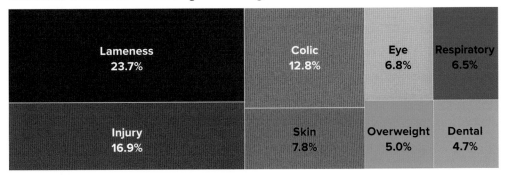

| Lameness 23.7% | Colic 12.8% | Eye 6.8% | Respiratory 6.5% |
| Injury 16.9% | Skin 7.8% | Overweight 5.0% | Dental 4.7% |

Source: 2015 USDA NASS Equine Health and Management Study in the United States
https://www.aphis.usda.gov/animal_health/nahms/equine/downloads/equine15/Eq2015_Rept1.pdf (8/2023)
*Other less common conditions reported: Digestive 3.4%, Underweight 2.7%, Reproductive 2.4%, Endocrine 2.3%, Cancer 2.2%, Behavioral 1.8%, Neurologic 1.8%, Other 1.2%, Fever/Undetermined Origin 1.1%, Other Infectious Disease 0.8%, Liver or Kidney Disease 0.7%, Pigeon Fever 0.4% – *Standard Error = 0.2%–1.1%*

Veterinarian Wendy Ray Miller preparing for an open castration procedure

VETERINARIAN

You need to have a good equine veterinarian. You will need veterinary care and advice. Find a Vet who you really get along well with and enjoy their company. Life is too short for strained relationships, and remember, oil and water still do not mix!

There are Vets who know horses but don't have people skills. Then there are Vets who are excellent horsemen, equine specialists, have outstanding people skills and make great friends. I hope you find one!

Get-A-DVM (Doctor of Veterinary Medicine)
The American Association of Equine Practitioners offers a database of their member-veterinarians, searchable by location, here:
>> *https://aaep.org/horse-owners/get-dvm*

❷ *Thumb Rule:* **AAEP is a good information source for most problems**

TRAINER

The big question is do you and/or your horse need additional schooling or training? As with most ventures, you need to constantly be learning just to stay even. To make progress, you need to seek and accept good training. Most all successful athletes today have their own personal trainer.

In looking for a trainer for you and your horse, you need to ask a lot of people who participate in your area of interest who the better trainers are. Eventually, you want to end up with the trainer that is best for you. As you start your quest, be aware that there are "many trainers but few horsemen". If the trainer you are investigating is not a horseman, drop them immediately. Do not get involved in an unworkable situation.

Trainer Stacy Westfall instructing rider Lisa Middleberg at a DQHA Horsemanship Camp in Gut Darß, Germany

Once you have identified a horseman/trainer it is possible that your personalities don't match. There's no need to pour your money and time into an oil and water situation. Oil and water simply don't mix; they stay separate. Keep looking! Your horseman/trainer needs to enjoy success in competitions. They need to have a reputation for high moral standards and honesty in their business relationships and in their communication with and treatment of both the horses and owners. They need to be empathetic, yet at the same time discipline the horse and offer admonition to the rider. They need to be financially solvent and good businessmen. Once you've found your person, you need to be fully aware of the costs involved.

❷ *Thumb Rule:* **Oil & water do not mix**

QUESTIONS FOR YOUR PROSPECTIVE TRAINER:

What is the monthly training fee for the horse? This is partially determined by whether or not the horse is boarded at the trainer's facility. It is probably best for your horse to be at your trainer's facility because the horse is always there and you are not responsible for the daily transportation of your horse.

How many days a week and generally at what time will your horse be ridden?

Is there an additional cost for training you, and when will you and your horse be given your training together?

Your trainer will evaluate your progress and your horse's progress and assist you in becoming proficient in your desired discipline(s). They will also be able to take you to competitions and assist you as you compete. All of this costs money. Just remember that time is money, and you are receiving the knowledge and experience that the horseman/trainer has spent a lifetime acquiring.

> ❷ *Thumb Rule:* **There are many trainers but few horsemen**

Having your horse trained is a little like buying an automobile over time: there are monthly payments that must be made. If you fail to make the auto payments, you lose your vehicle. If you fail to have your horse trained, you still have the horse and all the responsibilities. Your advantage is that your horse, when well trained, proficient and winning, is probably worth more money! However, when you sell your horse, you probably will not recoup all of your training expenses. The automobile is worth less every day you own it.

As you and your horse become more proficient, you may only need occasional tune-ups with your trainer to stay at the top of your game. Trainers understand and accept this, as their clientele has a normal turnover and they want you to be successful. Your success is the best advertisement your trainer can get! Today, most all winning athletes have trainers and coaches.

> ❷ *Thumb Rule:* **A good horseman/trainer can make your investment much more enjoyable and profitable**

SHOWING

Many will have no interest in showing. It is wonderful to have a great horse for trail riding, mountain trips, etc. – just a good pardner!

However, if your competitive juices push you into showing and you can afford it, go for it. Many people have found great fulfillment through their accomplishments in showing. There are local, state, national and international competitions in most areas of interest. The primary thing most horse owners receive from showing is satisfaction from within when you've trained hard, competed fairly and been rewarded with a championship. Championships are not the singular goal. There is only one championship trophy in a given class at each show. Horse show buckles can be very costly! The camaraderie, lifelong friendships and personal goals determined and realized – all of these things make life really worth living.

Today, many of the leading exhibitors are female and compete in the **amateur division**. Amateur generally denotes a person who is past the age of 18 and does not receive money or remuneration for training, judging, giving lessons to others, or showing someone else's horse. The definition varies according to breed or group, so you need to be specific for your breed and interests. It's your responsibility to know your breed's rules. Once the amateur status is violated or taken away, it can take years for reinstatement. The major advantage of the amateur status is that you do not have to compete against professional trainers. However, as an amateur, you may still also compete in open classes against the pros!

Every breed and/or competition group has an annual rulebook you can download that details in depth all breeding, registration, transfer, and show rules and regulations. Stay abreast. If you do show, make it fun and be successful. For instance, if you are second in a class of only two entries, you can say, "I was second, and Joe (who won the class) was next to last!" Or you can simply say, "I was runner-up in the class".

> ❷ *Thumb Rule:* **Nothing says you have to show in order to enjoy your horse**

Jacinda Roybal & VON MORE ROUND showing in Ranch Riding at the AQHA World Show

The author with daughter-in-law Linda, son Josh & wife Rusty enjoying a trail ride through Soledad Canyon in the Organ Mountains – Las Cruces, New Mexico

TRAIL RIDING

So you have your horse and you have no interest in showing or wish to take a break from showing. This is not a problem; you will find many other horse owners who share your opinion. Trail riding and just enjoying being with your horse is great therapy and enjoyment. You can easily find others who want to do the same. A trail riding horse does not require the same amount of training and high-dollar equipment as the show horse.

A good trail horse must be well trained, and you will need help from a horseman/trainer as you get started. A good trail horse must be broke, calm, know how to cross water safely, not easily frightened and be willing to go wherever you ask him with little resistance. He does not have to be as "highly tuned" as a competitive show horse. Enjoy riding the trail horse in God's marvelous creation. You will not be disappointed.

The author returning to the campsite after taking his horses to water – Kaycee, Wyoming

PACKING & OUTFITTING

You and your horse have become one. You're well experienced at trail riding and have been to a few shows. Now for a new, more exciting adventure: **Horse Packing!**

What is horse packing? An oversimplification would be putting your camping gear in a pack on the back of a horse, getting on your horse and taking off to explore God's Creation for a day, a week or more.

Your first experience should be with a professional horse packing outfitter or with a friend who is experienced and has all the needed equipment. You should probably ride the outfitter's horses on this first trip, and they will also have mounts for your friends to join you! Sitting atop a good horse, you will experience the countryside and landscape from a completely different view.

Naturally, if you are to be gone for more than a day, you will need camping gear and food. A professional outfitter will supply these. You will need to choose the location you wish to ride and experience. Your leaders will have good ideas for a route that is not too rough for you and your horse, if you decide to take him on this first trip. Follow their advice and suggestions.

National Forests have excellent trails and camping sites. Better yet are our fabulous Wilderness Areas. A designated Wilderness Area is a large mass of land that has been set aside by the U.S. Government for foot travel by horses and humans only. Motorized vehicles and tools are prohibited in these areas. National Forests allow motorized toys and equipment. This is what sets the Wilderness Areas apart and makes them more peaceful and less crowded.

In addition to the actual packing, there are many things to consider. Be certain there is water and grass near your camping area. How will you take care of your horse at night? We normally use high, tight rope lines between trees. We never tie our horses overnight to a tree. The horse will stomp and damage the roots of the tree and over time it will die. This is exactly what we do not want to happen.

Horses tied to a highline strung 7-8 ft high between sturdy trees in the Pecos Wilderness, NM. In this photo, the horses' lead ropes have been extended in order for them to eat off the ground. After eating, they will be raised and tied at normal head height for the night

Four-horse packstring heading to Lily Park, Gila Wilderness, New Mexico

Earlier in the book, hobbles were mentioned on page 68. Your horse should be hobble-broke so that during rest periods and once you have unsaddled at camp, he will be able to graze. On these trips, the horse will need to graze a minimum of 3-4 hours a day. Don't think your horse can't run away with hobbles on! They can and without injuring themselves. Always keep one horse tied so you can go find the others in case they wander or run off. I tell you these things from experience – the world's best teacher!

Various Hobbles: Twisted Latigo, Chain, Double Ring & Braided Cotton (DIY from Leadrope)

Some packers will take a portable electric fence. They work well, provided all your horses are trained to use an electric fence. Again, keep one horse tied.

The author pulling the lash rope tight on a "Double Diamond" hitch, securing a canvas top pack over hard panniers at Willow Creek Ranch at the Hole-In-The-Wall

A good horse can carry about 12.5% of his body weight: 1,000 lb. horse = 125 lbs of gear, or 1,200 lb. horse = 150 lbs. of gear. A good pack mule can carry 15% of his body weight. The pack horse/mule is carrying dead weight. Your riding horse is carrying live weight, which moves with the horse in a helpful manner.

Horse Packing Equipment

Lash rope & cinch, canvas or poly tarp (also called a "manta") to cover the load & keep it dry, soft canvas panniers & hard plastic panniers (pictured slung on sawbuck pack saddle), & scale

The panniers for carrying the gear should be balanced within 1.5 lbs of each other – a must! The cinches and pack ropes need to be as tight as you can get them. Even so, you may have to re-tighten them on the trail.

Pack Saddle Rig

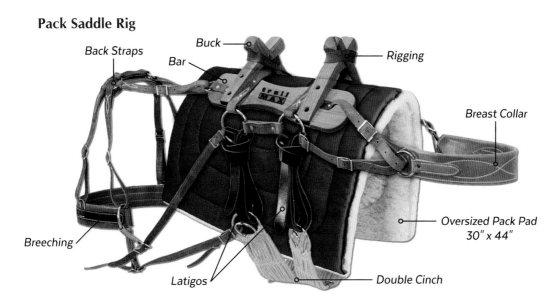

Back Straps
Buck
Bar
Rigging
Breast Collar
Breeching
Oversized Pack Pad 30" x 44"
Latigos
Double Cinch

Commonly used "Sawbuck" pack saddle by TrailMax™ (outfitterssupply.com)
with breast collar & breeching to prevent slippage on ascents/descents
Photo courtesy of ©Outfitters Supply, Inc | TrailMax™ Pack Saddle made by Russ Barnett

Read books, study the pictures, find a good outfitter and take a two-three day first trip. If it pushes your button, you might just buy another horse and pack equipment and learn to really enjoy our wonderful country. The horse you purchase for your pack horse can also be used for friends to ride.

There are three musts to remember:

1. If you pack it in, pack it out – leave no trash
2. Always leave your campsite in better condition than you found it
3. An experienced person in your group should carry a firearm

There are many books on packing. One that has a lot of comic relief and excellent information is one of the oldest, "Horses, Hitches and Rocky Trails", by Joe Back (Skyhorse Publishing). The University of Wyoming published a "Packing and Outfitting Field Manual" by Oliver C. Hill (Pioneer Printing) that to this day is still the simplest and most practical book I know of.

Photos ©Skyhorse Publishing & ©Pioneer Printing

119

TRAVEL WITH YOUR HORSE

Some states require brand inspection certificates to prove ownership when traveling with your horse. Regulations vary from state to state.

In New Mexico, you must have a **Brand Inspection Card** when you haul your horse. Brand Inspectors hired by the NM Livestock and Sanitary Board are responsible for these inspections. You either have to have your horse inspected every time you haul him or purchase a permanent brand inspection card that stays with the horse as long as you own him. Many states do not require brand inspections; check with your state vet (*https://usaha.org/saho*) for the requirements in your area, or follow the link and enter your trip itinerary for a list of required documents: *https://www.interstatelivestock.com*.

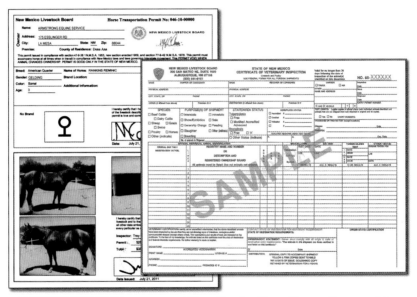

RANKIN REMINIC'S permanent New Mexico Brand Inspection card & sample Certificate of Veterinary Inspection form for intrastate travel

For interstate transport, you need a **Health Certificate** from your Veterinarian. Health Certificates (also known as a Certificate of Veterinary Inspection) are usually only good for 30 days. The negative Coggins test documentation (good for 6-12 months) is part of the Health Certificate.

❷ *Thumb Rule:* **Keep your paper work current and with you when traveling with your horse**

It is a good idea to practice loading in several different types of trailers. Before going on a long trip, you need to have a trailer that has:

- ❷ Good Tires
- ❷ Good Floor
- ❷ Good Hitch & Safety Chains
- ❷ Lights & Brakes
- ❷ Proper License
- ❷ Insurance

If your trailer is a two-horse side-by-side, you should load your horse on the left hand side. If traveling with two horses, the heavier horse should be on the left. This is because most highways have a slight upward slope to the left or center of the road, and this will aid in keeping things balanced and pulling smoothly.

If you're hauling a stock trailer with large open pens, you should tie your horse(s) to the left side. They will tend to have a 45° angle for balance. Some commercial horse vans have pens that require the horse to ride facing backwards. This is no problem for the horse. If you notice larger stock trailers going down the road with a horse that is not tied, the loose horse will often be facing backwards!

On long trips the question always arises as to how often you should stop and let your horse out of the trailer. Some people stop and let the horse out every 2-4 hours. Many horses, when you let them out, won't drink water. They just want to nibble grass if it is available. You are going to be stopping every 2-4 hours for fuel and restrooms. This stopped period gives the horse time to relax and refresh without being unloaded.

Most travelers give their horses access to hay in built-in feeding bunks or hay bags. This allows the horse that is used to being hauled to go all day without being unloaded. Many horses are difficult to reload, plus you may not have a good area to let them out. But if time is of no issue go ahead and find a good place to unload, water, feed and exercise your horse on your trip.

If you are overnighting on your trip, plan ahead and secure stabling. There are horse people in most areas that offer overnight boarding, which you can locate on the internet (i.e., *https://horsetrip.com*). Traveling with your horse requires time, expense and planning, but is a wonderful opportunity for both of you.

COSTS

This brings us to the age old question, "Do figures lie or do liars figure?" Anytime we write down figures and costs that are meant to be averages, they are good for only a given period of time.

The worksheet on the next page lists some potential annual expenses. Costs can vary as much as ±20% depending on your geographic area and unexpected situations. You can wear out 2-3 pencils and several yellow legal pads as you calculate costs.

Let's consider the cost of keeping your horse under two different scenarios:

① You own the farm and are doing it yourself

② Using a full service boarding facility

The costs for both systems are very similar. Do-It-Yourself has advantages but more headaches. The Full Service Boarding affords you, as a horse owner, fewer interrupted nights and much less stress and physical work.

Full service boarding facilities generally range from $300-$800 per month, with $450 being the average. Some demographic areas are higher. At full service facilities, you are still responsible for vet, farrier, grooming, clippers, fly spray, etc., which amount to roughly $1,920.00 annually or $160 per month.

There will always be additional cost factors. Training, if needed, will range from $500 -$1,500 per month; the average = $1,200 including board.

The above figures do not include a saddle or horse trailer, whose costs vary widely according to personal wishes. There is a difference between needs and wants. There is nothing wrong with fulfilling your wants if your finances can accommodate your desires.

Saddle: The purchase of your saddle is a big ticket decision. The right saddle is essential for a comfortable and enjoyable ride. Prices vary widely: $750–$5,000.

❷ *Thumb Rule:* **The right saddle is paramount to enjoying your horse**

ANNUAL EXPENSE COMPARISON WORKSHEET	DO-IT-YOURSELF	FULL SERVICE
BOARDING	✕	
FEED		
HAY		✕
GRAIN		✕
SALT/MINERALS		✕
HEALTHCARE		
BEDDING		✕
VETERINARY (VACCINES, EMERGENCY/FIRST AID, ETC.)		
FARRIER		
TEETH FLOATING		
GROOMING (BRUSHES, FLY SPRAY, ETC.)		
EQUINE HEALTH INSURANCE POLICY		
TACK & EQUIPMENT		
WATER & FEED BUCKET		✕
HALTER & LEAD ROPE		
SADDLE & PADS		
BRIDLE, REINS & BIT		
WINTER BLANKET		
APPAREL (BOOTS, SPURS, HELMET, ETC.)		
PROPERTY		
UTILITIES (WATER, ELECTRICITY, ETC.)		✕
MAINTENANCE (BARN, FENCES, ETC.)		✕
PASTURE MAINTENANCE (IRRIGATION, FERTILIZER, ETC.)		✕
WASTE DISPOSAL (MANURE)		✕
MACHINERY MAINTENANCE (TRACTOR, IMPLEMENTS, ETC.)		✕
INSURANCE		✕
TAXES, CAPITAL DEPRECIATION, INTEREST, ETC.		✕
HIRED FARM LABOR		✕
TRANSPORTATION		
HEALTH CERTIFICATE, COGGINS TEST, ETC.		
VEHICLE & HORSE TRAILER (MAINTENANCE, TIRES, ETC.)		
TRAINING/LESSONS		
SHOWING (ENTRY FEES, TRAVEL EXPENSES, ETC.)		
ASSOCIATIONS (MEMBERSHIP, REGISTRATION)		

123

Ed's heeling horse, BABE, watching the beavers play in Snowmass Creek, Colorado – 10,120 FT

It is vital that the saddle fit both the rider and the horse. Saddle sizes are indicated in inches. This measurement is from the back of the swells to the cantle. A 15 or 16 inch seat fits average sized adults. Not only the seat length but also the seat shape and width must be comfortable. Sit on the saddle and hopefully ride it before making your decision. Ride a few minutes in as many of your friends' saddles as possible to determine what style and size fit you best. This is one of the benefits of purchasing a good used saddle. Different equine events are more easily accomplished in certain saddle styles.

Trailer: Your choice, just be certain your vehicle is heavy and powerful enough to pull and stop the trailer safely. Bumper pull trailers (as opposed to goosenecks) enable you to travel in your car; you are not restricted to a pickup truck. Trailers can cost as much as your first house. Many living quarter trailers today may qualify under the tax code as second homes. Check this out with your CPA if you are so inclined. You will seldom find a good, safe, second hand trailer for less than $5,000.

Miscellaneous expenses can easily add another 10% to your total. Don't hesitate to buy second hand tack and equipment, especially when you're just getting started. After all, the horse you just purchased is "second hand"! You can always step up in class once you know exactly what you need and want.

> ❷ *Thumb Rule:* **Save money & shop for quality used tack**

Finally, **manure removal**! Stall cleaning is a time consuming and daily job, but somebody has to do it! The healthy horse drops a load of feces about every two hours. We call it feces before it hits the ground; then it becomes manure.

You feed your horse approximately 4 tons of feed (dry matter) annually, and your horse presents you with about 10 tons of manure. Before you panic, the manure is roughly 80% water. But it still has to be hauled away! The manure can be stored in a stack and composted to be used on farm fields, pastures, gardens, flower beds, etc. Just remember, you need a means for getting rid of it. Try to find farmers and gardeners who will come pick up your manure pile and use it on their fields. Getting rid of it can be burdensome and expensive.

Nutrient Content Estimates of Horse Manure (lbs/year*)

Nitrogen (N)	Phosphate (P_2O_5)	Potash (K_2O)
110 lbs	59 lbs	110 lbs

Secondary nutrient content of horse manure includes Magnesium, Calcium, Sodium & other Micronutrients

Our 1,200 lb horse will fill this 7.5 ft³ wheelbarrow about 50 times per year! (~1 ft³/day)

*Nutrient content estimates based on an 1.100 lb horse.
Source: Livestock Waste Facilities Handbook, MidWest Plan Service (1993)

Armstrong Equine Service in La Mesa, New Mexico

HORSES & LAND AS A BUSINESS

Anytime you consider developing a business, you need to consult with a good CPA, and preferably one who knows something about the horse industry. Most of the financial increase in the horse business comes from land appreciation over time. Land bought at a good price is almost always a good investment. The important thing is the value of the land you purchase, not the cost.

We are often reminded of the three most important factors in real estate: ① Location, ② Location, ③ Location! Knowing the demographics of the location you are considering is critical because eventually the property you purchase will be resold. Position yourself properly.

One of the quickest and perhaps easiest ways to get into business is to purchase an existing horse facility in a good real estate location. There are usually older horse facilities for sale in most every area. Some are available because of retirement, others due to empty nest or divorce, but many are due to failure to be profitable.

The IRS basically gives your business seven years to show a profit if you are operating as a business. Most horse owners are not operating as a business. Even so, use the word "hobby" lightly and infrequently. The IRS and all government programs are constantly changing, so be certain you and your CPA have and follow all current rules and regulations.

> ❷ **IRS Farmer's Tax Guide** » *https://www.irs.gov/pub/irs-pdf/p225.pdf*

Demographic Estimates of U.S. Equine Uses & Breeds – USDA NASS 2015

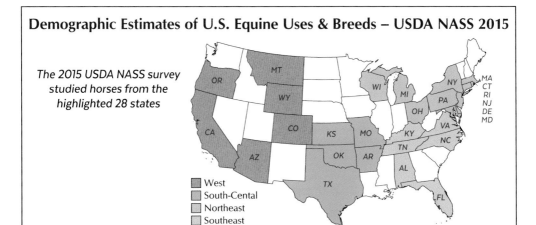

The 2015 USDA NASS survey studied horses from the highlighted 28 states

West
South-Cental
Northeast
Southeast

Primary Use of Horses	U.S. Total	West	South-Central	Northeast	Southeast
Pleasure	47.2%	37.7%	46.5%	44.6%	58.6%
Farm or Ranch Work	25.0%	36.6%	28.8%	23.3%	11.2%
Breeding	8.5%	8.6%	8.8%	8.0%	8.3%
Showing/Competition	8.1%	7.7%	7.6%	7.3%	9.8%
Retired/Not In Use	4.7%	4.3%	3.5%	6.1%	5.4%
Lessons/School	3.2%	2.1%	1.8%	5.9%	3.6%
Racing	1.6%	0.2%	2.1%	2.6%	1.2%
Other	1.8%	2.8%	0.9%	2.3%	1.8%

Breed Distribution	U.S. Total	West	South-Central	Northeast	Southeast
Quarter Horse	42.1%	55.5%	61.8%	21.7%	21.4%
Thoroughbred	7.1%	4.2%	2.4%	10.1%	13.7%
Paint	6.8%	7.4%	8.0%	6.4%	4.8%
Miniature Horse	5.1%	2.3%	5.0%	6.3%	7.1%
Draft	4.7%	2.2%	1.1%	15.2%	2.5%
Tennessee Walker	4.5%	1.1%	0.7%	2.1%	15.1%
Arabian	3.9%	4.2%	2.3%	3.9%	5.9%
Standardbred	3.7%	1.1%	1.4%	10.7%	2.9%
Warmblood	3.2%	2.1%	1.6%	5.2%	4.4%
Saddlebred	2.5%	0.9%	2.8%	1.8%	4.3%
Appaloosa	1.9%	1.8%	1.6%	2.5%	2%
Morgan	1.4%	1.5%	1.0%	2.9%	0.6%
Mustang	1.0%	2.0%	1.1%	0.5%	0.4%
Other Breeds	7.8%	9.3%	4.2%	6.7%	12.3%
Grade	4.1%	4.5%	5.1%	4.0%	2.5%

Note: Data collected from a stratified random sampling of 3,997 equid operations from 28 states, representing 70.9% of U.S. operations with ≥5 equids (horses, ponies, mules & donkeys), & 71.6% of the U.S. equid population based on the 2012 USDA Census of Agriculture.

Source: https://www.aphis.usda.gov/animal_health/nahms/equine/downloads/equine15/Eq2015_Rept1.pdf (8/2023)

Boarding facilities are generally more profitable than breeding programs because they have a steady cash flow. Breeding programs require more capital and take several years before you have offspring to sell. Breeding programs also require more expertise in different management areas.

If your horse interest has been centered around your child, there often comes the time when they may outgrow their interest, become more interested in boys or girls (heaven forbid), or go off to college. The time, companionship and money you have invested in your youth may well be the greatest return on any investment you have made or will ever make. This may be the time for you, the parent, to step up and into horse competition. You will have gained much knowledge as a horse show mom or dad, driver and entry fee financier. Horses are also great for a midlife crisis. Or you can sell out to another new horse enthusiast or experienced exhibitor. Or you may want to become a horse breeder. If so, read on.

Let's consider a boarding facility. Assume you find a nice facility near your town and would like to own it. If you have the capital or the ability to acquire a mortgage to purchase the facility, you are ready for business. Another approach if you are not financially able to jump right in but are known to be honest, forthright and a hard worker is to lease the property with the option to purchase it by a given date as far in the future as you can negotiate with the owner.

2017 Direct Economic Impact Estimates of U.S. Horse Industry by Sector (AHC)

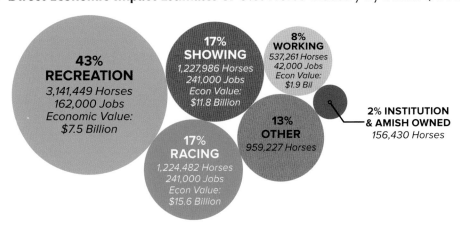

American Horse Council - *https://horsecouncil.org (8/2023) 2018 Economic Impact of the Horse Industry, page 10*

The lease option sets the price you will have to pay but gives you time before you have to come up with all the money. Hopefully, this land is appreciating in value every year. If the property appreciates rapidly or you have the opportunity to sell at a profit, you can exercise your option to purchase the property and to sell it at that same time.

We will assume your leased property has a house for you or the person who will manage it for you. After a little clean up, you are in business. Paint is the cheapest improvement. All of the repairs you have to make are tax deductible expenses, and major purchases are depreciable items. Good records are crucial.

> ❷ *Thumb Rule:* **Paint is the cheapest improvement**

Once you exercise your option and purchase the facility, you can then itemize fences, wells, barns, houses, etc. and put them on appropriate depreciation schedules. Your expenses and depreciation are taken away from your gross income to arrive at your taxable net profit. Most times in the early years, your operation will probably operate at a loss. This horse loss can generally be written off against your income from other non-horse activities and result in a lowered tax burden for the year in question. Keep your CPA informed.

The goal is always to make a profit. Just remember, you never escape taxes. When you shelter them, you are only delaying them. Depending on the political party in power, you will have more or less opportunity to be entrepreneurial. When you finally sell the facility, you will be subject to capital gain taxes on the increase in value of the property.

Another aspect that can sometimes work with the lease/purchase agreements is to ask the owner for a release clause that will allow you to sell part of the land at any given time for a previously specified value per acre. Then you can sell another person acreage, pay down the final purchase price, and hopefully make some money for yourself while still maintaining enough acreage to continue a successful horse operation.

> ❷ *Thumb Rule:* **Keep your CPA in the loop - try not to tangle with the IRS**

Purchasing land and building your own horse facility is another option. This allows you to build according to your plans and desires, but usually takes more time and is more expensive than purchasing an existing facility. But you have the satisfaction of having a facility that meets your personal aesthetic desires and physical layout. This is important.

Be sure to involve proper, experienced counselors/advisors when building, buying, and/or starting your own business. Count your costs first, and then proceed. Most small businesses go under due to undercapitalization.

A boarding facility is the simplest way to get into business. Starting a breeding program is a long-term endeavor that requires a great deal of capital and management. While difficult, there is no greater reward in the horse business than breeding, raising, training and showing your own champion!

The author & his stallion COMMAND N CHEX showing in Reining at the National Western Stock Show in Denver, Colorado – 2008

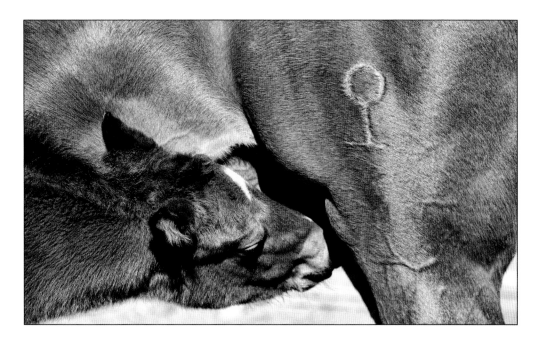

BREEDING YOUR MARE

The horse you purchased for your daughter or son was a mare, and now they are no longer interested in horses. What do we do with the mare? You, as the parent, may have become seriously interested in horses and would like to keep her as your own personal horse. Or you might like to breed her and raise a foal. Both of these are good situations. The third option is to sell the mare and retire from the horse industry. Options one and two are more exciting!

Another situation, not as favorable, is that the mare becomes injured and must be laid off from riding for a year or so. "Tincture of time" is often the best medicine for full recovery. You can consider breeding the mare and raising a foal during this period of time.

You have purchased a nice mare, and she has proven to be a good athlete. Therefore, a foal by the right stallion should be a fine opportunity to give you a whole new set of equine experiences. This foal should be reasonably easy to sell, or you can keep it for your next riding horse. Remember the Thumb Rule: "**Inferior mares should never be allowed to reproduce**". This is the reason you spent so much time and effort purchasing a good mare at the start of this adventure. Read more about Reproduction in Part 5 on page 169.

Linda Pummell and Rusty enjoying driving Welsh Pony TRIANA

ENJOYMENT & PERSONAL SATISFACTION

These are the major keys. This means that you must keep your financial obligations intact. Being behind on your board bill, vet bill, feed, farrier, etc. will make your horse ownership a nightmare (no pun intended). You will soon become discouraged and sell out at a very low price just to get out of debt.

This is why planning ahead is so very important. It doesn't help anyone in the chain when you fail. If you've made a mistake with the horse you purchased, the boarding facility you've chosen, or your trainer, admit it sooner rather than later and make the changes that will keep you happy and successful.

Again, the purchase price of the horse is just the **tip of the iceberg!**

> ❷ *Thumb Rule:* **It's your program and money so position yourself to enjoy it to the max**

U.S. Congresswoman Yvette Herrel & RANKINS REMINIC talking politics with the author

LAST BUT NOT LEAST

It is very important that we, as horse people, do not allow our government to designate horses as **companion animals** or anything other than **livestock**. Should this happen, we will never be able to enjoy these magnificent creatures as we now do. **Horses must remain as livestock!** It's important to be politically involved if you want to keep the freedoms you presently enjoy.

If horses become designated as companion animals, you will no longer be able to depreciate them in your business plan and you may have to register them within your city codes. The less government entanglement, the better! Be active politically for the sake of enjoying the Wilderness and mountain trails, and fight to keep horses from being designated companion animals.

Horses are livestock. Enjoy yours!

Photo ©Jim & Fran Combs Collection

"You can see what man made from the seat of an automobile, but the best way to see what God made is from the back of a horse."

—Charles M. Russell

Circa 1880s, the *"Original Cowboy Artist"* Charlie Russell, mounted with packhorse somewhere in Montana. Russell lived the life he so masterfully captured in a collection of over 4,000 paintings, sculptures & writings. Courtesy of the © Jim & Fran Combs Collection

Josh Armstrong breaking & training a two-year-old *VON REMINIC* filly for Dogie & Joyce Ann Jones of the Hashknife Ranch, Watrous, NM

RIDING YOUR HORSE

Contributed by J.H.B. "Josh" Armstrong, Jr.

You now own your horse, your horse is broke to ride, and you are ready to ride! There are several important steps you need to follow before every ride.

WARMING UP

When you first get your horse out, before you get on, you need to be sure your horse is not too fresh. Snap a 25 ft rope to his halter and chase him in a 40 ft circle at a trot with a lunge whip, or work him in a roundpen (see page 71). If he volunteers to lope, run, or buck, that is okay. Just keep him going the same direction until he finds the trot.

When he has trotted a couple of circles ask him again to lope a step. If he wants to lope more, that's okay. When he has trotted a couple of circles, ask him again. When he's ready to ride, he will lope off without expression and lope less than a circle before finding the trot again. If you want to lunge him in the other direction, that's fine. If you want to save the other direction until tomorrow, that's also fine.

Older horses may not require this much warm-up and should be ready to mount after grooming and saddling.

GROOMING & SADDLING

Tie the lead rope to the hitching rail with a slip knot that can be easily released in case of an emergency. It is a good idea to wrap the lead rope around the rail two times before tying the slip knot (see page 57). In the event your horse sets back, this will make the knot much easier to untie.

> ❷ *Thumb Rule:* **Never allow someone to mount or sit on a horse that is securely tied!**

Walk all the way around your horse and examine him thoroughly for any possible injuries. Brush off the body, mane and tail completely. Be especially sure to thoroughly clean the horse's back and underline where the saddle and cinches will go. Always brush in the direction the horse's hair lies. This prevents uneven spots under the pad/blankets that may cause back sores when the horse is ridden. Sores on the back are slow to heal, and you won't be able to ride your horse in this condition. Use your hook pick and carefully clean all four hooves (see page 60).

Metal & Rubber Curry Combs & Mitt, Stiff & Soft Bristle Brushes, Hoof Pick & Mane/Tail Comb

Now you are ready for your saddle pads. Be certain there is no trash or dirt on the underside of your saddle pads and blankets. Always put them a little too far forward. This way, as they slide backwards, or you slide them backwards, they will keep the hair on the back smooth and flat. Use only as many pads/blankets as you need. If your horse has good, prominent withers, he will only need one or two. Too many pads/blankets make it difficult to keep the saddle in place without having to cinch your horse overly tight. Lift the pads up in the front center to relieve pressure on the withers. Cinching the horse too tightly tends to make them irritated and may cause them to be extremely difficult to cinch up in the future. I cinch the horse three times: barely snug the first time, a little tighter after putting the bridle on, then cinching tight before I get on.

If your saddle has two cinches, always tighten the front first and the rear second. If you are using a saddle that you have never ridden before, this is a good time to check the stirrup length. Place your fingertips at the base of the swells, and with your other hand, pull the stirrup up to your armpit. The bottom of the stirrup should rest gently against your armpit. Make the necessary adjustments, shortening or lengthening as needed.

Lifting pads up to relieve pressure on withers

Trainer Darryn Lackey checking stirrup length

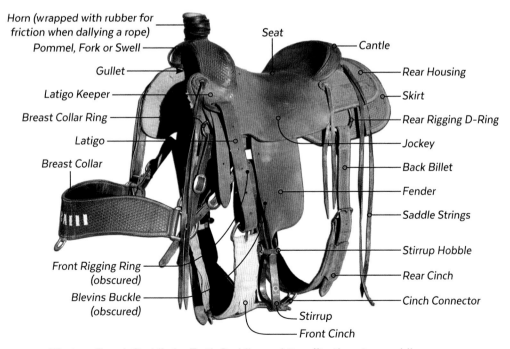

Horn (wrapped with rubber for friction when dallying a rope)
Pommel, Fork or Swell
Gullet
Latigo Keeper
Breast Collar Ring
Latigo
Breast Collar
Front Rigging Ring (obscured)
Blevins Buckle (obscured)

Seat
Cantle
Rear Housing
Skirt
Rear Rigging D-Ring
Jockey
Back Billet
Fender
Saddle Strings
Stirrup Hobble
Rear Cinch
Cinch Connector
Stirrup
Front Cinch

Western Ranch Saddle by Truth Saddlery – *https://truthcustomsaddlery.com*

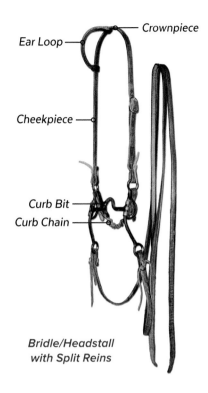

Crownpiece

Ear Loop

Cheekpiece

Curb Bit

Curb Chain

Bridle/Headstall
with Split Reins

Herman Middleberg bridling his horse at a DQHA
Horsemanship Camp in Gut Borken, Germany

Once the saddle is secure, it's time for the bridle. You should always be careful and slow when handling the horse's ears and face.

① Untie the lead rope and buckle the halter around the horse's neck. Never leave the horse tied while the halter is buckled around the neck! Keep ahold of the lead rope so you don't lose your horse.

② Arrange the bridle in the direction that it will go on the horse.

③ Hold the crown piece with your right hand and the bit with your left.

④ Lift the crown piece up to the poll of the horse's head, and with your left hand, carefully insert the mouthpiece of the bit into the horse's mouth. Never bump his teeth or be too quick or forceful when inserting it into the mouth.

⑤ It may be necessary to apply pressure with your thumb (on your left hand) on the side of the lower lip to encourage the horse to open his mouth and accept the bit. Be slow and patient, this has to be done every time you want to ride.

Kay Wienrich searching for the right bridle in his tack room – Spabrücken, Germany

⑥ Slip the crown piece over the right ear and then over the left. Gently slip the ear into the adjustable loop, if the bridle has one.

⑦ Make sure the bit is in the correct position – adjust the length of the headstall so the bit just touches the upper corners of the horse's mouth.

⑧ Release halter and place it in a safe place, you'll need it again when unsaddling.

⑨ Take both reins in your right hand and lead your horse away from the hitching rail. It is best to first move your horse at a 45° angle to the hitching rail. This causes him to move his front feet more easily, and he is less apt to refuse your command to follow. You should lead from the left side, and your right shoulder should be opposite the horse's head.

⑩ At the arena or wherever you are going to ride, it is a good practice to turn your horse around you in a tight circle a few times in each direction before mounting. This seems to get the kinks out of a horse and make him quieter to mount and ride off.

MOUNTING

Be sure your cinch is tight enough. Lead your horse a step or two after tightening the cinch. It is a good idea to turn him 2-3 tight circles to the right and the left "to get the kinks out".

Hold the reins in your left hand. When mounting from the left side, the left rein should be tighter than the right and should have light contact with the horse's mouth. Standing at the shoulder, grab a hand full of mane with the reins in your left hand. With your right hand, turn the stirrup toward you, and ① put the ball of your left foot in the stirrup. Always get up before you get on. ② Stand up in the left stirrup with both your legs on the left side of the horse. Keep your reins short in your left hand and your right hand on the saddle horn. If you like the way things look, ③ sneak your right leg over and into the right stirrup.

When mounting, if your horse does not stand still and wants to move forward, a good habit is to pull him in a circle to the left. This allows centrifugal force to help you find your seat in the saddle.

FIRST THING

Always ride with the ball of your foot on the stirrup and your heels down. It's going to be natural for your foot to keep sneaking too deep into the stirrup. Keep shaking it back and reminding the ball of your foot to stay on the stirrup.

Pull softly on both reins until your horse backs up a step. When he backs a step, put your hands down in front of the saddle horn so he gets release from the bit pressure and he knows he did the correct thing.

When that's too easy, do the same thing but say the word "whoa" first. That word means back a step, whether you're running, standing still, trotting, whatever. When you say the word, push your heels forward and lean your shoulders back.

When that's too easy, push your hands forward, squeeze your legs or bump him gently, maybe cluck a little, and walk him off. Now from the walk, push your heels forward, lean your shoulders back, say the word "whoa" and back him up a step.

When you like the way he's standing, still on slack, ask him to walk and then do it again. When you're comfortable you can go a little further, and maybe faster, before you tell him the word again. I don't stop a horse. I simply stop going forward and begin backing up. Learn to back your horse a step or two every time you stop going forward.

> ❷ *Thumb Rule:* **Don't stop – transition from forward into backing up**

Georgia Criss Armstrong transitioning VON CHERRY *from the lope to backing up*

As long as you know that you can get him stopped and backed up, you will feel confident to try new things. But it is important that both the horse and rider recently backed up and have that back up on their minds. Ride your horse for 20-40 minutes at all of the gaits you are comfortable with.

A horse is like a loaded gun. And you never know when it's going to go off. When something unexpected happens, you need to be ready to get him stopped. If he doesn't stop when you pull, pull harder. If he still doesn't stop, pull even harder. If he still doesn't stop, pull more harder. Pull hard enough to get the job done. Then you can regroup and decide what to do next. There is a huge difference between pulling and jerking – **never jerk**!

DISMOUNTING

As you finish your ride, you need to get off safely. You are going to dismount on the left side, so the first thing you do is take your left foot almost out of the stirrup. Hold both reins short with a handful of mane in your left hand. Keep the left rein slightly shorter so you can turn him under you if he decides to move forward. Hold the saddle horn with your right hand. While looking at the horse's head, stand in your left stirrup, swing your right leg behind you and step down.

If needed, you can use a mounting block to both mount and dismount. Be sure your horse will stand still for the whole process, or have someone hold him for you.

Take a moment to ensure you have your balance. Then take both reins off the neck and lead your horse back to the hitching rail.

> ❷ *Thumb Rule:* **Never get on or off, or sit on your horse without the reins in your hands**

UNSADDLING

Buckle the halter around your horse's neck and remove the bridle. Be patient and let the horse "spit" the bit out as you lower the crown piece. Never pull the bit from the horse's mouth. Now put the halter on, buckle and tie it to the hitching rail.

If using a breast collar, remove it first. Then remove the rear cinch (if one is used) and then the front cinch. Fasten your cinches to the saddle so that they don't fall off on the ground and get dirt or trash on them. Remove the saddle and blankets together in one motion. Replace your bridle, saddle and pads back in the tack room.

Brush and/or curry your horse well while examining him for any nicks or cuts. Rinse him off with cool water during hot weather. Pet him, thank him for a good ride, and return him to the pasture, paddock or stall. Remember to turn him around before you unhalter, then back away so he can run, kick up and play (see page 56).

Darryn Lackey rinsing off RUBI after unsaddling

TRAINING

To bond with your horse more quickly, it is helpful to understand how your trainer has taught the horse. I train a horse in 3 stages to do 5 things:

3 Stages:	5 Things:
① Initiate Motion	① Forward
② Maintain Motion	② Give the Head
③ Challenge Motion	③ Backward
	④ Give the Shoulder
	⑤ Give the Hip

I always ask the horse nicely once. I never ask the horse nicely twice. I ask him as hard as I ask my iPhone. If I ask harder than that, that is what I call begging, and I never beg. And I ask the horse as long as I touch my iPhone when I want it to do something.

So, I ask the horse nicely once; then I bump him, bump him, bump him until he decides I should quit bumping him with my legs (not my spurs). I bump him hard enough to make him uncomfortable, but not hard enough to make him scared. For most horses, this means I bump him as hard as a fly hits him when it lands on his body. We've all seen a fly move a horse.

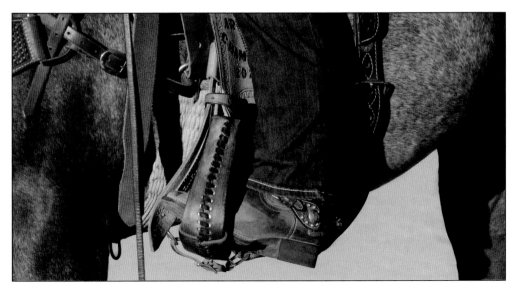

Bump with your leg, not your spur

148

Trainer Mario Castro teaching two-year-old VON MANY LETTERS to move forward at the La Union Ranch – open spaces are great places to allow a horse to learn to go forward

1. FORWARD

So, to move a horse forward I touch the horse with my pant leg, then bump, bump, bump until the horse decides I should quit bumping him and shows me his decision by moving forward.

The most valuable transition is the stand still to trot transition. I work all of my upward transitions the same way, including the slow walk to fast walk, the slow trot to the fast trot, and the lope to gallop.

Once the horse is initiating the desired gait decently, I work on maintaining that gait. I set myself a goal to keep the horse going at that gait until I get to a chosen fence post. When accomplishing that goal becomes too easy, I set myself a further goal.

> ❷ *Thumb Rule:* **Forward motion is the start of all training followed by yielding to pressure, voice commands, hands, legs & weight-shifting**

2. GIVE THE HEAD

The second thing I teach a horse is to give his head. This is most easily done in a snaffle bit. To ask for the head to the left, I hold both of my reins in my right hand, with the tail of the left rein on the right side of the horse and the tail of the right rein on the left side of the horse.

Then I reach my left hand down the left rein closer to the bit, and I put a pressure on the horse's mouth as hard as a fly landing on his nose. With my right hand on his mane to stay out of the way, I hold the pressure on the left side of the horse's face towards his tail until he decides I should let go and shows me his decision by moving his chin to the left.

❷ *Thumb Rule:* **This exercise is the basis of everything I will do with the reins in the future**

3. BACKWARD

The third thing I teach a horse is to back up. To back a horse, I draw straight back toward my elbows with both reins, harder and harder, until the horse decides I should let go and shows me his decision by moving a foot back. I ask by pulling on the reins. When he says "yes" by moving a foot backward, I say "thank you" by releasing the pressure on the reins.

When I first ask the horse to back up, his question to me is, "Why should I?" My answer to him is, "Because I will let go of you when you do". Eventually, the horse will get through the "why" stage. He won't remember why he backs up when I pull on him; he will only remember that he has always backed up when I pulled on him. Then I can keep pulling on him, and he will keep going backwards.

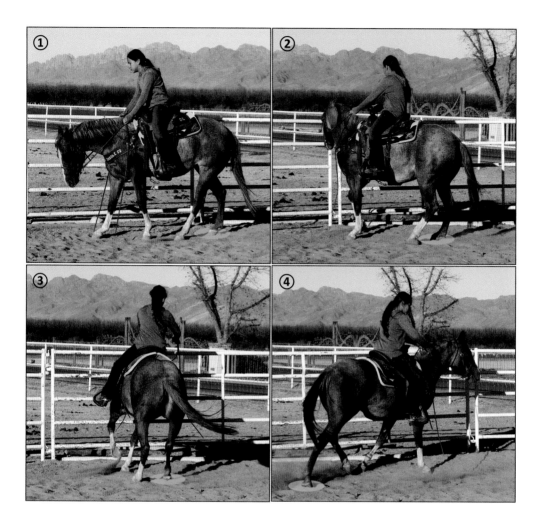

4. GIVE THE SHOULDER (ROLLBACK)

The fourth thing I teach the horse is to give his shoulder. The maneuver I use to teach this is the rollback. With the horse walking parallel to the fence ① I back the horse a step, ②/③ turn him toward the fence ④ then move him off in the same tracks he came in on. If he does it correctly, his back feet will stay still in the turn, and his front feet will walk around them.

The goal in the rollback is to keep the front feet moving. They're going forward, then they are backing, then they are going forward again. I try to back as slow as possible, turn as slow as possible, and leave as early as possible.

5. GIVE THE HIP (TURN ON THE FOREHAND)

The fifth fundamental I teach a horse is to give his hip. The exercise I use for this is the turn on the forehand. I am going to ask the horse to walk his back feet around his front feet.

To move the back feet to the left, I first open my left leg by locking my left knee. Then I move my right leg back behind the back cinch and push. If pushing doesn't work I bump, bump, bump until the horse decides I should quit bumping and moves a rear foot to the left. As I do this, I draw the horse's head around to the right for balance. My goal as I push the hip to the left is to keep the right front foot from moving. With these five fundamentals, I can get a horse to do anything.

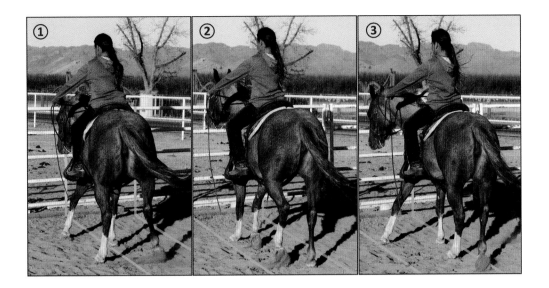

SIDEPASS

One of the first examples of combining these fundamentals into maneuvers is the sidepass. To introduce the sidepass, I walk the horse straight up to a fence that he cannot put his head over. I have already taught the horse to give his front feet in the rollback and to give his back feet in the turn on the forehand. Now I'm going to ask him to move both the front feet and the back feet at the same time.

It is my hands job to keep my saddle pointed at the fence. To sidepass right, I first open my right leg by locking my right knee. Then I push with my left leg in the middle of the horse's side until the horse takes a step to the right. If pushing doesn't work I bump, bump, bump until the horse decides I should quit bumping.

As I continue to combine these five fundamentals into more and more advanced maneuvers, I ask myself two questions after each exercise: "Can I get the same response without looking at the horse?" and, "Can I get the same response with less pressure?" Those two questions are what I use to continue to advance my horsemanship as well as my horse's performance.

> ❷ *Thumb Rule:* **All parts of the horse's body must be trained to move or yield independently**

Photo adapted from ©Shane Rux Photography

2018 Reserve Champion Versatility Ranch Horse Stallion VON GUS in the right lead

LEADS

When a horse lopes, he always leads with one foot. The horse should always lope on the inside lead. Which is to say that when he is loping to the right, his right foot should be leading his left foot.

The first step in learning to catch the inside lead is to speed up at the trot when the horse is turning. When the horse goes fast enough, he will naturally take the inside lead as he goes into the lope.

The second step is to ask the horse to speed up into the lope from the trot in one step. To do this, I move my outside leg back behind the back cinch and squeeze. If he does not lope I bump, bump, bump until the horse says, "Quit bumping me". He says this by loping.

Correct Leads are critical for speed & balance especially through tight turns –
Barrel Racing horse trainer Haley Gilliland competing in San Antonio, Texas

If a horse has trouble taking the inside lead in either of these steps, it is because:

1. He is not straight, and
2. He is not going when I tell him to; he is going after I tell him to like my computer does, rather than when I tell him to like my wheelbarrow does.

In either case, I skip on to the next step which is loping from a walk. The horse has to lope off in one step. The horse has to know exactly which step I want him to lope on. So I cue him very clearly by:

1. Squeezing him behind the back cinch with my outside leg,
2. Pushing my hands, shoulders and chin forward, and
3. Clucking

It is easier for a horse to understand exactly which step he is supposed to lope on from a walk than it is from a trot. But if he has trouble with that, I go on to the next training step anyway, which is loping out of a rollback.

At this point, my horse already knows how to rollback at a trot. I will be trotting along one yard from the fence and parallel with it. I tell him the word "whoa", back him a step, turn him toward the fence, and lope off in the new direction. My goal in this exercise is to back as slowly as possible, turn as slowly as possible, and lope as early as possible. At the midpoint of this rollback, the horse is positioned to most easily lope in one step.

Once he can lope out of a rollback easily, it will be easier for him to lope from a walk without trotting. Once he can lope from a walk without trotting, it will be easier for him to lope from a trot in one step.

LEAD CHANGES

A lead change is the act of picking up a new lead from the lope, rather than from the walk or trot.

A horse lopes with an inside arc to his body. If a horse is loping straight down a road in the right lead his head will be to the right of his shoulder, his shoulder will be to the left of his head and to the left of his hip, and his hip will be to the right of his shoulder. So, when I ask a horse to change from the right lead to the left lead, I first put a left arc in his body. I do this by sidepassing him to the right. A right sidepass will normally cause a left arc in the horse. When I have the left arc, I move my right leg behind the cinch and squeeze the horse into the left lead.

The cadence of the lope is the most important factor in a successful lead change. In a right lead, the horse's left rear foot hits the ground first. Then his right rear and left fore hit the ground at the same time. Then his right fore hits the ground. Then all his feet come off the ground for a moment in a period of suspension.

The easiest time for the horse to get all his feet changed around is during this period of suspension. The longer the period of suspension, the easier it is for the horse to change leads. The easiest way to increase the period of suspension is to lengthen the stride. The easiest way to lengthen the stride is to go faster. So, I normally introduce the lead change at a strong cadence.

Josh Armstrong & VON Gus loping in the Right Lead with a Left Arc approaching a Period of Suspension to change into the Left Lead

Photo ©Lori Gardner

CATTLE

I teach a horse 3 things regarding a cow:

    ① **Go with the cow**
    ② **Stop with the cow**
    ③ **Turn with the cow**

Most of my time is spent teaching the horse to keep the cow from getting back to the herd of cattle. Which is to say, playing defense rather than offense. I back the horse one step often. This trains the horse to anticipate rocking his weight back onto his rear end. This enables his front feet to move freely.

I usually cut one cow out of a herd of cattle. But even when I am only working one cow without a herd, I still practice the same positions. When I cut a cow out

Eddie & RANKINS REMINIC cutting a Corriente cow from the La Union Ranch

of the herd, my goal is to keep the cow from getting back to the herd and to find a chance to let my horse stand still. If the cow can see the herd, my horse is in the wrong position. If the cow cannot see the herd, my horse is in the correct position.

I never ride toward the cow, I always ride toward a point that is between the cow and the herd. My goal is not to chase the cow. My goal is to cut the cow off at the fence. I turn toward the cow so the horse can keep an eye on the cow. I back up a step before I turn. I encourage the horse to back as slowly as possible, turn as slowly as possible, and then go as fast as it takes to beat the cow to the fence.

As with all horsemanship, my goal is not to do more. My goal is to do less and allow my horse to do more.

BITS

There are two classes of bits: **snaffles** and **curbs**. Snaffles have rings. Curb bits have shanks. Snaffles work on direct pressure. Curb bits use leverage. Curb bits are not good for green horses because they have a slapping action that can hurt the horse and make him want to decide right now what he is going to do.

Loose Ring Snaffle   D Ring Snaffle   Eggbutt Snaffle

A snaffle does not pressure the horse as much, so he has more time to think about what he should do to get that pressure off his mouth. Snaffle bits are ridden with two hands in competition.

A less experienced rider should generally use a curb bit because it is important that the rider be able to apply a sufficient amount of pressure to get the horse stopped. Curb bits must be ridden with only one hand in competition.

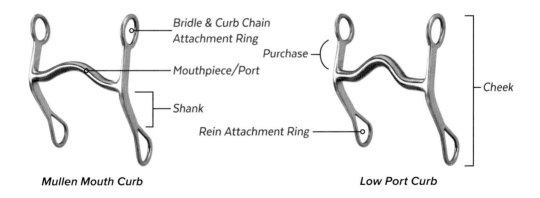

Mullen Mouth Curb   Low Port Curb

Curb bits vary in severeness and action based on the length of the shank, the length of the purchase (the purchase is the part of the shank above the mouth piece), the angle of the shank, and the type of mouth piece. Curb bits also have a leather or chain curb strap, which creates leverage.

The bit may hinge in a variety of places. Generally speaking, the more places the bit hinges, the more able the rider is to help the horse. The more solid the bit is, the more able the horse is to balance on the bit. So, with a stiffer bit, you don't have to help the horse as much, but you are also not able to help the horse as much.

For most riders and most horses, the first bit they should buy is a shanked snaffle. This gets even more confusing: A shanked snaffle, though it has "snaffle" in the name, is classified as a curb bit because it has shanks. The word snaffle in the name refers to the connection in the middle of the mouthpiece.

Tom Thumb
Shanked Snaffle

Loomis
Shanked Snaffle

Correction Bit

The shanked snaffle is a good compromise in that it can create enough pressure to stop the horse without scaring him. From there, a rider may choose to graduate to a more severe bit or to a stiffer bit, depending on the needs of the rider and horse.

The hackamore or bosal is not a bit. It has nothing in the horse's mouth. Many trainers use it to start colts, instead of a bit. AQHA rules state that a horse 5 years of age and younger (referred to as a "Junior" horse) may be ridden with a hackamore, snaffle, or curb bit. Horses 6 and older (referred to as "Senior" horses) may only be ridden with a curb bit.

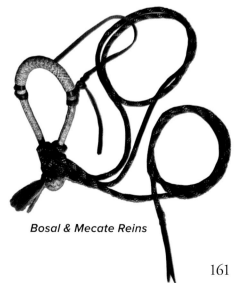

Bosal & Mecate Reins

SPURS

Spurs are like a dog – you don't have to teach them to work, you have to teach them when not to work.

Spurs are generally used as a correction rather than as a cue. Before a rider uses spurs, they should have a strong enough leg position to keep the spurs pointed at the ground when they don't want to use them.

Spurs should not be used on a horse until they are not needed to get the horse to go. In other words, spurs are reserved for horses that have already been taught to go forward.

To make a horse go forward, I always ask him nice once. I never ask the horse nice twice. I ask the horse nicely then bump him, bump him, bump him, bump him…until he decides I should quit bumping him by going forward. I bump him hard enough to make him uncomfortable, but not hard enough to make him scared. Often, that is as hard as a fly hits the horse when the fly lands on the horse's side.

It is not natural to go when someone pokes or kicks you in the belly. It is natural to bend over and feel sorry for yourself. It is natural to go when someone chases you with a rope or a bridle rein.

On a young horse, I ask him to go by touching him with my pant leg, then I bump him, bump him, bump him with the upper calf of my leg until he decides I should quit bumping him. From the second kick on, I also start hitting him with the bridle rein, again, hard enough to make him uncomfortable but not hard enough to make him scared.

Over time, the horse learns to anticipate that the bridle rein is coming, and he chooses to go before it comes. After more time, the horse learns to anticipate that the kick is coming, and he chooses to go before it gets there, too.

Then one day the horse knows he is supposed to go, but he just doesn't want to go right now. That is when I add the spur.

Photo Francie Jones Photography

Joe III demonstrating strong leg position riding VON METALLIC ROAN with spurs pointing down

I don't use the spur often, but it is always available. When the horse knows I will spur him, that is when I don't have to spur him. Spurs encourage well broke horses to increase their response time when performing maneuvers.

SUMMARY

HORSEMANSHIP:

- Helmets are a good idea!

- Leg and foot position are the foundation upon which all riding and training maneuvers are based – **Heads Up & Heels Down!**

- There should be a straight line through the rider's elbow & hand to the bit

- Elbows should never be behind your back

- The rider's head should always be up and eyes looking forward, or in the direction you are going. The horse will always be between your legs, unless you have fallen off!

- Remember what your instructors have taught and shown you. Practice and use this good information every day

TRAINING:

- Back up immediately every time after stopping. This teaches the horse to use and stay on his hind quarters, ready to work, and keeps him from walking forward after stopping. Don't stop – just cease going forward and start going backwards

- Never jerk your reins to stop, or to do anything else – pull but do not jerk!

- Always keep your inside hand slightly higher than your outside hand when circling. This aids in keeping the inside shoulder up and makes lead changes easier and more natural

- The horse only has about a 15 minute attention span for training, don't overdo. Train for 10–15 minutes and then just ride. Later, train again for 10–15 minutes. Try to end on a good note

- While riding, correct your horse when it is needed, but do not fiddle with your reins all the time. Discipline and correction are necessary but should only be done properly and when needed

For more info, watch Josh's *1st Dimension* video here:
» *https://armstrongequine.com/the-first-dimension*

For questions, clinics, training, or to ride with Josh, contact him here: *https://josh.armstrongequine.com*

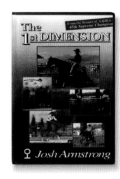

List of the 52 Supreme Champions out of the almost 7 million American Quarter Horses that have achieved a AAA Racehorse Speed Index and earned 40 points in Halter and Performance Classes at 5 or more shows under 5 different Judges with at least 2 Grand Champion Titles, 20 points in Show Classes & 8 points in Cattle Classes:

1967 – KID MEYERS
1968 – FAIRBARS
1968 – BAR MONEY
1968 – JETAWAY REED
1968 – MISS ROY DECK
1968 – CAT'S CUE BAR
1968 – ENHANCED
1970 – MACH I
1970 – MILK RIVER
1970 – GOODBYE SAM
1971 – DESTO BAR
1971 – ASTRO DECK
1971 – LEO MAUDIE
1971 – DIAMOND DIVIDEND
1971 – MY STORMY BOY
1971 – LIGHTNING REY
1971 – DIAMOND DURO
1971 – BACK STRETCH
1972 – MAGNOLIA PAY
1972 – HANK WILL
1972 – DECK JACK
1972 – DESTINY JAGETTA
1972 – SUGAR SABRE
1972 – LINDA SCOTLAND
1973 – GOLDSEEKER BARS
1973 – JOE FAX HORSE
1973 – BEATLE WIN
1973 – FIRE ROCKET
1973 – SUGAR ROCKET
1973 – GOLDIE BARS
1974 – JET THREAT
1976 – BAR H RAIDER
1976 – LITTLE TOWN
1976 – COLDSTREAM GUARD
1977 – WONDER SEEKER
1977 – SAVANNAH TIGER
1977 – TH DEMON
1977 – SAILOR'S NIGHT
1978 – COFFEE BAR KING
1978 – WESTERN OTOE
1979 – WAR MACHINE
1979 – SIR SAVANNAH
1979 – HE ROCKET
1979 – GOLDSEEKER BUD
1995 – GOTUM GONE
1997 – LUCKS EASYFANTA BOY
2008 – MR JOE IM COOL
2010 – CARTEL CALIENTE
2013 – FLY THE RED EYE
2014 – GOTTA GOOD HABIT
2014 – IMA REGAL CHOICE
2018 – BRTSENDINGMYREGARDS

Josh & GOTUM GONE owned by Catherine Carr – AQHA's 45th Supreme Champion

"I'm so glad that I was able to pass my love of horses on to my children... it's important for children to have a love of animals, and horses are such special creatures."

—First Lady Jacqueline Kennedy

November 19, 1962 – First Lady Jackie Kennedy & son John Jr. aboard SADAR with daughter Caroline Kennedy & her pony, MACARONI, riding at their Glen Ora estate in Middleburg, Virginia. SADAR, aka "BLACK JACK", was a bay gelding gifted to the First Lady by the President of Pakistan, Muhammad Ayub Khan.

Two month old colt VON COMODIN playing peekaboo

Part 5

REPRODUCTION

So you've decided to breed your mare! Here are some things you need to know. We will start with your mare and then go to the stallion.

First, with a mare there is no such thing as normal. The gestation period of a mare is 335-340 days, or 11 months and 1 week. With any biological entity, there is an accepted range of days. Plus or minus two weeks is not abnormal.

Male foals are normally carried 2-7 days longer than fillies. Foals born in warmer weather tend to have a few days shorter gestation than those bred to foal in the early winter months. Mares on a high level of nutrition tend to foal 4-5 days earlier than mares on a low nutritional plane.

Most breed associations use January 1st as the annual birthday for all foals born in that calendar year. A foal born on June 1st will be considered one year of age (or a yearling) on the next January 1st. This is the reason that most stallion services do not begin their breeding seasons before February 1st. A foal born on December 31st is considered one year of age on January 1st!

When a mare is referred to as being in **estrus** (or heat), it indicates that she is receptive to the stallion for breeding. The mare's **estrous cycle** is normally 21-22 days. Mares tend to be seasonally polyestrous. However, in colder climates, mares often go into anestrous where they are not sexually active. As the days get longer, they become polyestrous and cycle every 21-22 days.

The estrous cycle is divided into two parts: ① **estrous period**, when the mare is sexually receptive to the stallion, and ② **diestrous period**, when she is not receptive to the stallion. The normal length of estrous, or sexual receptivity, is 5-7 days, with diestrous being 15-17 days. Most **ovulations**, the release of the egg from the ovary, occur 24-48 hours before the mare goes out of estrus.

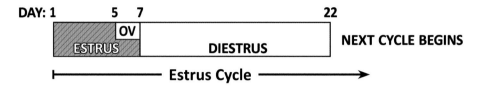

The mare needs to be in a healthy state of nutrition – good flesh but not gobby fat. It is difficult to get thin, malnourished mares in foal. Mares that are not in a good nutritional state need to be gaining weight for breeding to be successful. Mares that are well fed and fleshy do not need a special diet when breeding. Stay with your balanced diet of high quality nutrients in adequate amounts.

The choice of stallion that you want to be the sire of your foal needs to be decided at least a month before you wish to breed your mare. As you research stallions, you will see Breeding or Stallion Fee, and a few other annotations. Example:

> Breeding Fee = $2,500 LFG
> Booking Fee = $500 (Not Included)
> Mare Care = $18/day DRY or $20/day WET

The **Breeding** or **Stallion Fee** is the fee you will pay the Stallion owner for your prospective foal. LFG is "Live Foal Guarantee". You are guaranteed a live foal, defined as one that "stands and nurses". After this, the death of your foal is no longer covered by the LFG. If your foal is stillborn or dies before nursing, you must get a veterinarian to write a letter to the stallion owner attesting to the death. This allows you to breed your mare to the same stallion the following year without paying an additional Breeding Fee.

A **Booking Fee** is charged by most stallion farms. It may or may not be included in the Breeding Fee (read closely). The Booking Fee assures you that you will be able to breed your mare to your chosen stallion in the correct year. The Booking Fee generally goes to the farm that is handling the stallion and not to the stallion owner, unless they are one and the same. The Booking Fee is non-refundable. Should your mare not conceive or have a dead foal, you will have to pay another Booking Fee the following year when you take advantage of your free Live Foal Guarantee.

Mare Care is the daily fee you will pay the farm where your mare has been taken for breeding. This covers her daily feed and care. **DRY** is for a mare that does not have a foal with her. **WET** is a mare that has a foal at her side. WET mares require more feed and attention.

It is my thought that in most of the USA, it is not necessary to have a foal born in January unless you have a heated barn and a good staff of workers. Most foals born in March do just as well in competition as those born in January and February. The only exception to this is for breeders that are raising foals that will be shown at halter as weanlings in the late summer or early fall of their birth year.

Foals born at the beginning of spring seem to have fewer illnesses and really get off to a good start. The natural design for the mare was to foal when grass was beginning to be plentiful so that she could produce adequate milk to grow a healthy foal, have enough nutritional energy to maintain her body, and be ready to breed back for the next year's foal. In colder, snowy areas, May and June foals may be preferable. Use common sense.

Mare & nursing foal on lush pasture owned by Marcus & Cindy Rensing, Nordenau, Germany

You know your mare, now let's look for a stallion. Stallion services are more available than ever, with semen shipping opportunities available from all over the world. You have several breeding opportunities. The first and oldest is **pasture breeding**. You take your mare to the stallion owner, and he turns her loose in the pasture with the stallion and other mares. Pasture breeding works well but is more dangerous for your mare since she is suddenly introduced to a strange group of mares. You understand female congeniality! Other more acceptable breeding programs are:

Hand Breeding: Your mare is taken to the stallion owner's facility and when she is ready to breed, the stallion is brought to your mare.

Shipped Cool Semen: You can keep your mare at home and have the breeding Vet or technician check her with an ultrasound machine to determine when she should be inseminated. This requires several ultrasound visits and hormonal injections to be certain that your mare is ready to ovulate when the semen arrives.

Your Vet or technician will order the semen for overnight delivery for breeding the next day, after they've calculated that she will ovulate the next day. Then they will check the following day to see if your mare has indeed ovulated. If she has not yet ovulated, you inseminate again and check for ovulation the next day. Most, but not all, stallion owners will ship you two doses of semen to breed two times. If you did not receive two semen doses or if the Vet/tech feels insemination is imminent, you may be able to have semen collected and flown to the airport nearest you for same-day insemination.

It has been my experience that, on average, it requires two shipments for a pregnancy. Some Vet/techs are better than others, some mares are more fertile than others, and some stallion's semen is better than others. We expect the average stallion's cooled, shipped semen to be viable for ±2 days.

If your mare was being hand bred at the stallion owner's facility, she would be checked daily to detect estrus. Once your mare shows strong heat (estrus) for three days, the stallion will breed her and continue breeding every other day until she is no longer in estrus.

Regardless of the method of breeding or insemination, your mare should be checked at about 16 days post-ovulation for pregnancy. Should she not be pregnant, you will begin to go through the same process again. Remember, each estrus cycle is about 21 days. 16 days post-ovulation means she should be back in heat in a few days if she is not pregnant.

You get the good news that your mare is pregnant at the 16 day check! In a week, have her ultrasounded again to be certain that she is still pregnant and that your embryo has a heartbeat. Check again at 45 days and then relax. Your mare will need her regular balanced ration of feed.

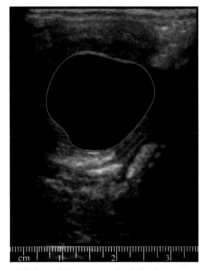

16 Day Ultrasound of Embrionic Vesicle in the Uterine Horn approximately 25 mm in diameter

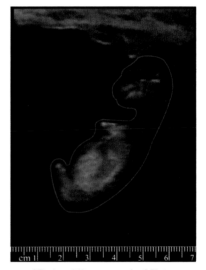

45 day Ultrasound of Fetus in cranial body of Uterus approx 50-70 mm in length

Breeding with Frozen Semen: Frozen semen has the advantage that you or your Vet/tech already have the semen when your mare is ready to be bred. Again, she will have to be ultrasounded several times.

One disadvantage to frozen semen breeding is that all stallions' semen does not freeze well. This is also the case for cooled, shipped semen. Try to learn in advance about the stallion's cooling and/or freezing status. A second disadvantage is that you or your Vet/tech must be able to properly handle frozen semen, i.e., have a liquid nitrogen tank to store it in.

Johanna Schulte holding mare in palpation chute, used for horse & handler safety during reproductive examination, pregnancy diagnosis and artificial insemination

If you have limited frozen semen, it is generally recommended to ultrasound your mare every 6 hours for signs of ovulation, starting when your Vet/tech believes she is close. Once she has ovulated, thaw the frozen semen and inseminate her. Basically, you are dealing with a 6 hour window.

With frozen semen, we are inseminating based on a known time of ovulation. Whereas with cooled, transported semen, we are inseminating based on a hopeful time of ovulation.

As you have already figured, breeding with cooled, shipped or frozen semen adds additional expenses, but it enables you to breed to the stallion of your choice. Cooled, shipped semen will run between $300–$750 per shipment, and frozen semen will probably be at the upper end of that range. The mare owner is also responsible for the cost of returning the semen container. Most semen shipping is done via FedEx, UPS, courier, or airline. Don't get caught financially off guard.

Once your mare has been diagnosed to still be pregnant at 45 days, she can live a normal life until foaling. It is a good idea to continue riding your mare for her exercise and your enjoyment. She can be ridden and shown for the next ±6 months, but decrease the amount as time progresses. Keep your mare current on her vaccinations and deworming programs.

Two weeks before the foal's due date, you need to have things ready for foaling. Your Vet needs to be put on standby. Unfortunately, most foals tend to be born between 2 and 4am!

Decide whether you want your mare to be allowed to foal in the pasture or in a stall or pen. With mares having their first foal, the stall or pen is preferable because when foaling starts, it goes in a hurry!

A few days before foaling, the mare's udder will have enlarged and the teats will become very large. The mare is making and preparing to deliver milk for her foal. One to two days before foaling, you usually see a stream of wax proceed from the teat canal and accumulate into an inch-long string. This is nature preparing the udder and teats for milk production. The wax will break off and may appear again. Often, you will see some milk drip from the teats the day before or the day of foaling, as seen below.

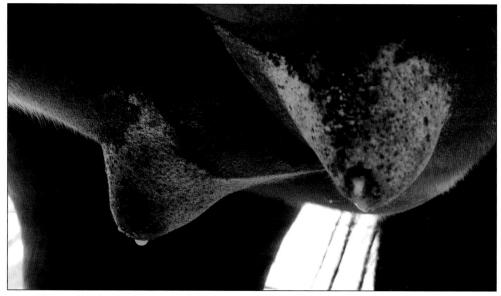

Waxy, dripping teats are a telltale sign that foaling will likely occur within 1-2 days

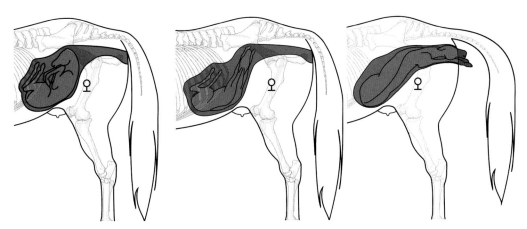

Stage 1 of Parturition with the foal gradually rotating into position in the birth canal in preparation of expulsion with the contractions of Stage 2

The foaling process is known as **parturition** and is broken into three stages:

Stage 1: The mare becomes nervous, gets up and down, begins sweating (starting behind the ear and moving rearward), has cramps, and her first water breaks. This ends Stage 1. Stage 1 can last from a few minutes to several hours.

Stage 2: The mare will lay down hard, get up, lay down again, and begin pushing to expel her foal. Soon you will see a white bag (allanto-chorionic membrane) and the appearance of feet. It is critical to notice the position of the feet to be sure it is the front legs that are coming out. Stage II goes very rapidly, so you need to be ready and have all the necessary help you might need.

Hopefully, you will see one front foot ahead of a second front foot and then the nose. The above mentioned sequence is necessary in order for the shoulders to easily pass through the birth canal. This should only take 5-15 minutes.

Then suddenly the foal is out. The back legs may still be in the mare. If both the foal and mare lay quietly, there is no need for you to do anything at this point unless the membrane is covering the foal's nostrils and mouth and preventing it from breathing. If so, quietly step in and remove the membrane and move back out. It is good for the mare and foal to lay quietly without either one jumping

Oxygen-rich blood flowing to the foal through the umbilical cord, still intact

up and breaking the umbilical cord. There is an amount of oxygen-rich blood that can be transferred to the foal at this time. I love watching the mare and foal lay there and begin to recognize one another. The miracle of God's Creation!

Stage 2 should only last up to 20 minutes. If the mare does not really start pushing early and hard, it could go up to an hour. This is when you need your Vet or help readily available. You may have to manually pull the foal out of the mare.

Stage 3: The expulsion of the afterbirth (placenta) should occur within 3 hours of birth. If not, consult your Vet on the means of removing the retained placenta. Spread the placenta out and make certain all parts of it have been expelled. Retained placenta parts can cause a mare to "founder" or have laminitis. Stage III is complete.

A difficult birth is termed **dystocia**. What is described above is an easy, normal birth. Occasionally, the foal's birth presentation may not be normal and have to be repositioned in the mare. This is when you really need help!

Photo courtesy of ©University of Wisconsin Madison

Knot tied in placenta to prevent it from being stepped on

After foaling is complete, the mare may show mild signs of colic for an hour or so. If it does not become severe, ignore it.

Again, be sure the nostrils are clean and the foal is breathing. The navel stump should be dipped (not sprayed) in a 10% iodine solution. I prefer filling a small jar with the 10% iodine and, with the foal standing, immerse the navel stump in the iodine for 5-10 seconds. An unattended navel stump is an excellent pathway for infection and navel ills. If the mare is up to date on vaccinations, there is no need to administer additional vaccinations. However, some farms do administer a prophylactic dose of antibiotics and vaccines. Again, have a good relationship with your Vet.

The foal should stand and nurse within 30 minutes. If the foal is not and nursing within 2 hours of birth, it should be helped up, held, and positioned to get milk from the mare's teats. This is easier said than done, but it is of utmost importance for the foal to receive the mother's **colostrum** – the first milk that is rich in antibodies and has a laxative effect. Colostrum antibodies are only absorbed by the foal's digestive tract for 36 hours, and the mare only produces them for 48 hours.

Within up to 12 hours, the foal should have a bowel movement of **meconium**, or fetal excrement. Its shape reminds me of a Tootsie Roll! This is very important, and if the foal doesn't pass it and is straining, it will need an enema and/or other treatments. Always look for the Tootsie Roll, 6 to 12 inches in length.

I like to give foals a Fleet Phosphate enema at 12-24 hours of birth. They are inexpensive, ready to use, and may be helpful.

NORMAL FOAL VITAL SIGNS

99.5°-102.1°F
(37.5°-38.9°C)

80-100
BPM

20-40
BREATHS
Per Minute

Excitement, air temperature & foal's size/age will affect normal vital signs

Check the foal's eyelids to be sure they are not turned under. This condition is called **entropion** and does not occur often. If it exists, roll the eyelids out and apply an eye ointment. Some foals occasionally have to have a stitch to keep the eyelid rolled out.

Diarrhea in a foal can dehydrate, cause serious problems and lead to death in a matter of hours. Call your Vet. The only time not to be concerned about foal diarrhea is when the mare is in foal heat.

Foal heat usually occurs 8-12 days after the mare gives birth. The mare is unique in that she is capable of breeding back this soon after giving birth. The first regular estrus occurs 21 days after foal heat, or about 30 days after birth. Most mares are rebred in this first regular heat and will produce their next foal on about the same date as the present foal.

If your mare is foaling later in the year and you wish for her to foal earlier, you can speed her up about three weeks by breeding her on foal heat. Three things must have happened before you consider breeding on foal heat: first, the afterbirth should have been passed within 3 hours after foaling; second, the mare has no tearing or bruising of the reproductive structures; and third, there is no infection or abnormal uterine discharges.

If you have decided not to breed your mare again, she is referred to as "open". Or, you may breed your mare and she does not get pregnant, or she may get pregnant and later absorb the embryo. This, too, results in an open mare.

Mustang mare and foal moving on 30 minutes after giving birth

It is best if your mare and foal have a nice pasture in which to grow and play. Your mare will need some grain or sweet feed in addition to the pasture or hay she receives. Feed her enough that she milks strongly and does not lose weight. Feed 5-8 pounds of grain, depending on the quality of the pasture. You may also wish to feed the foal. Just be sure your foal doesn't get too fat. This might cause your foal to develop joint and leg problems.

> ❷ *Thumb Rule:* **Sunshine and exercise are the best medicine for the average foal that is healthy & structurally correct**

Most foals are **weaned** at 5-6 months of age. By this time, the mare's milk production has decreased, and the foal needs additional nutrition. It is good to put the foal on a **creep feed** 4-6 weeks before weaning. A creep feed is fed to the foal in a place or manner in which the mare cannot get the foal's feed. The creep fed foal will already know how to eat grain when weaned from the mother. Breeders that want to show their foals at halter as weanlings may wean their foals as early as 3 months of age.

Weaning can be done by taking the foal a distance from the mother or by putting them in pens next to each other. In either case, the foal needs a secure stall or paddock to minimize the risk of injury while undergoing the weaning process.

It is best not to feel sorry for the mare with her swollen udder and let the foal nurse her during the weaning process. It is best to stop feeding the mare grain to allow milk production to slow down and finally stop on its own.

During the weaning period, put a halter on your foal and handle it daily. With the lead rope, just pull the foal from side to side; move the front feet to each side. If you attempt to lead the foal forward before it learns to move the front feet from side to side, he or she will probably pull back and turn over backwards. This can easily damage the head and neck. If the foal does start to go over backwards, hold the lead rope high and go back with him to keep the head from hitting the ground. You only need to handle the weanling 5-10 minutes. Don't overdo it!

In a few days, your foal will be leading. Do not leave a halter on the foal overnight unless the halter has a breakaway feature on it (see page 64). You don't want your foal to get the halter hung on something that might cause injury or death. Besides, putting the halter on and off daily is good training.

Weanlings often develop annoying or bad habits that need to be stopped immediately, or they will become worse with time. The first is nibbling and/or biting. When this occurs, immediately slap the weanling on his muzzle – don't be too gentle! The slap must be done immediately. Waiting and thinking about it first does not work. Be certain not to hit the eyes. The second is kicking at you. Take the lead rope, and while pulling the weanling in a circular motion around you, spank his hind leg with your lead rope. Don't be gentle with your slap, but don't overdo it. 1-2 slaps is sufficient. Take care of this before it becomes bad. Your weanling might also develop the habit of rearing up and striking with its front feet. Use the same procedure as for kicking, but on the front legs or chest. Always pull toward you, and never get directly in front of or behind your weanling.

Enjoy watching your foal grow and develop – it may be the breed's next champion!

Photo ©Will Rogers Memorial Museum

"There is something about riding down the street on a prancing horse that makes you feel like something, even when you ain't a thing."

—Will Rogers

Circa 1920 – *"Oklahoma's Favorite Son"* Will Rogers with his kids: Will Jr., Mary & Jim, enjoying a ride down the street, likely on their 20-acre ranch in Claremore, Oklahoma. A cowboy & gifted humorist, Rogers became the highest paid star in Hollywood, acting in over 70 movies & writing more than 4,000 nationally syndicated newspaper columns. Hugely popular, he became a world figure, speaking & entertaining as he traveled around the globe before his untimely death in an airplane crash in Alaska in 1935.
Photo Courtesy of Will Rogers Memorial Museum, Claremore, OK

The author & his first horse BEAUTY roaming the streets of Coffeeville, Mississippi

IN CASE YOU WONDERED

About the Author by Ed Armstrong

Joe – Joseph Hill Bates Armstrong, Sr. – was born in rural, small town Coffeeville, Mississippi on July 23, 1937. He enjoyed a typical childhood with wonderful parents, sister and brothers. Joe spent a lot of time with his maternal grandfather, who was a country doctor and farmer.

Elbert Sides became his first mentor at a young age. Elbert was a cattleman and horseman. In 1953, Elbert went to Tokio, TX, to learn the cutting horse business from three time NCHA World Champion Phil Williams (Skeeter, 1950 and 1951, and Little Tom W, 1952).

Elbert came home with a cutting horse gelding named "Buck". Buck may have been the first legitimate cutting horse east of the Mississippi River.

Later, Elbert married Joe's sister, Ann, and they let Joe go to major livestock and horse activities with them. Elbert made Joe score every horse they watched in competition and never said a word unless Joe had missed one. They also stood by the gate and watched every halter horse walk into the ring. Elbert always told him what he did not like about each horse.

Years later, when discussing horses with Rusty, she asked Joe, "Don't you ever find a horse you like?" His reply was, "If there was nothing wrong with one, I like him". This was a learning experience, and Joe became more positive in his evaluations.

Joe (left) & his brother's Fella & Ralph "helping" harvest hay on their Grandfather's farm in Skuna Valley, Mississippi – 1942

Joe with his first horse BEAUTY in Coffeeville, Mississippi – 1949

Joe's future brother-in-law Elbert Sides cutting on Buck at his farm in Como, Mississippi – early 1950s | Photo courtesy of Bonnie Sides

Left to right: James Calhoun on Ceasers Pistol, Andy Hensely on Poco Bueno, Milt Bennett on Poco Tivio, Phil Williams on Skeeter & Matlock Rose on Jessie James in San Antonio, TX – 1951

187

Trail Boss Joe leading the troops at the Philmont Scout Ranch in Cimarron, NM – 1955

Joe was involved in Scouting as a youth. Twice he went to the Philmont Boy Scout Ranch in Cimarron, NM, as a camper. Philmont is a 127,395 acre ranch that Waite Phillips gave to the Boy Scouts of America in 1938. In 1954, Joe hired on to work in the Horse Department. Philmont had 250 horses and 300 burros. To work in the horse department meant you had to help shoe and keep shod those 250 horses! It was a learning experience.

Armstrong entered the Cimarron 4th of July Rodeo. He was fourth in Saddle Bronc Riding, but they only paid three monies! Joe was the "mugger" in the Wild Horse Race, which their team won. A pattern was set!

Armstrong has a long and storied history in the livestock industry. He received a B.S. in Animal Husbandry at Mississippi State University, where he was a

Joe in the bareback riding at the inaugural MSU college rodeo, Starkville, Mississippi – 1959

member of both the Livestock and Meats Judging Teams. He then earned a M.S. from Oklahoma State University and a Ph.D. from Colorado State University, both degrees in Animal Breeding.

At Mississippi State, Joe formed a relationship with his professor, Carl Williams. Carl was a graduate of Texas Tech and was Joe's Livestock Judging Team Coach, and became his lifelong mentor. Later, as a professor, Armstrong attempted to emulate Williams' teaching methods and philosophies of education and life.

As President of the Block and Bridle Club, Armstrong and crew were responsible for organizing the first MSU Rodeo in 1959. Joe participated, but quickly realized he would never make a living rodeoing!

Philmont Scout Ranch – Cimarron, New Mexico

In 1955, Joe was responsible for leading 26 scouts and
leaders on 6 day horse packing trips over the ranch.
This was a weekly occurrence and turned out to be a passion.

In 1956, Armstrong was in charge of a camp with 75 horses, 72 saddles
and one wrangler. They took 60-70 riders out for a ride every day.

These years planted seeds that kept sprouting up at different stages in Armstrong's life.

Joe's college roommate, Ray Sewell, left, with professor & mentor
Carl Williams & Joe at the Mississippi State University Horse Farm

THE AMERICAN QUARTER HORSE ASSOCIATION

P. O. BOX 271 — 2736 WEST TENTH — AMARILLO, TEXAS

December 12, 1958

Mr. Joe Bates Armstrong
Box 5
Coffeeville, Mississippi

Dear Mr. Armstrong:

I am very happy to inform you that your grade, after attending the
Judging Clinic held at the University of Mississippi, was high
enough that you will have a No. 1 rating. This rating entitles you
to judge any size show.

It certainly was nice to have you in attendance, and we hope that
you profited by attending the School.

Very truly yours,

AMERICAN QUARTER HORSE ASSN.

Howard K. Linger
Secretary

HKL:dj

In the fall of 1958, Armstrong participated in an AQHA Judging Clinic at MSU.
At age 21, he was given the privilege of judging all size AQHA Shows

Bobby Rankin riding a bronc in Waco, Texas – 1954 | Photo courtesy of Trina Davis/Amy Rankin

Oklahoma State University was the next step. At OSU he met Bobby Rankin, who would also become a mentor and lifelong friend. Rankin, in addition to being very intelligent, was an excellent bulldogger (steer wrestler). He was the 1953 Reserve National Champion Steer Wrestler in the NIRA (National Intercollegiate Rodeo Association). Rankin also wrote much of the initial National 4-H Horse materials.

Colorado State provided many exciting opportunities. Joe was H.H. Stonakner's first Ph.D. student. In addition to loving the Rocky Mountains, three very important decisions were made at CSU. One, he met Rusty Vieh; two, he invited Jesus Christ to come into his life and become his Savior and Lord; and three, he convinced Rusty to marry him. He also received his Diploma!

Joe & Rusty selling Polled Hereford Cattle at Sunny Acres Ranch in Polk City, Florida – 1967

Armstrong's early career was in the beef cattle industry, while breeding and judging quarter horses. His first job out of the university was Extension Beef Cattle Specialist at Auburn University, Auburn, Alabama. In 1965, Joe judged the Central American Livestock Fair & Exposition with Rusty in San Salvador, El Salvador.

195

DERBY CENTROAMERICANO FUE GANADO POR CABALLO "EXITO" DE GUATEMALA. — Ayer en el Hipódromo de Las Colinas y en la 5a. carrera se efectuó el Derby y el Trofeo "Roberto Quiñónez S." se lo adjudicó el caballo EXITO, de Guatemala. El Pdte. de la Rep. coronel Julio A. Rivera felicitó al preparador norteamericano Mr. Jud Backer y al jockey J. Abel Rodríguez, por su eficiente trabajo en el redondel. FOTO DE ROY.

Rusty & Joe in a newspaper clipping after judging the Central American Livestock Fair & Expo. Pictured with friends Annabelle & Judd Baker, trainer of the winning racehorse EXITO, standing next to the President of El Salvador, Julio A. Rivera – San Salvador 1965

Legendary horse breeder & auctioneer, Hank Wiescamp, showing Joe his great broodmare SHIRLEY NICK at his sale barn in Alamosa, CO. As Auburn University Extention Livestock Specialist, Joe was helping select broodmares for cattleman & veterinarian H.B. "Woody" Bartlett to use in his breeding program in Montgomery, AL – 1966

Joe grooming stallion HEZA ROCKET who became Florida's first AAA+ AQHA Champion – 1969

Leroy Webb, Buster Welch & G.M. "Dogie" Jones – Photo courtesy of Miles Culbertson

On an Extension Service trip in 1966 with Alabama cattleman and cutter H.B. "Woody" Bartlett, Armstrong met Dogie Jones, owner of Hashknife Ranch in Watrous, NM. This, too, turned into a lifelong relationship. Joe and Rusty purchased their first broodmares (as weanlings) from Dogie and were introduced to Dogie's mentor, J.W. Shoemaker, an AQHA Hall of Fame Member. Mr. Shoemaker later sold them a stallion to breed to their mares.

Always having the desire to be in production agriculture, the next stop was Polk City, Florida. At Polk City, Armstrong developed and managed Sunny Acres Ranch, a large polled Herford cattle ranch with two AQHA Champion stallions and a band of twenty broodmares.

Joe also judged the National Polled Hereford and National Red Angus Cattle shows. Son Josh and daughter Criss were born in Florida.

R.B. Warren team roping with one arm on the National Senior Pro Rodeo Circuit – 2003

Armstrong showed and made HEZA ROCKET the first AAA+ AQHA Champion in Florida. Whenever "that one-armed judge from Nebraska" was judging a show (within 500 miles), he hauled HEZA ROCKET to the show. The "one-armed judge" never used him less than Reserve Champion Stallion. That man was R.B. Warren, who also became a mentor and lifelong friend. R.B. was missing his right arm below the elbow, but he was never handicapped! When he died at age 75, R.B. still roped and could tie-down a calf in 25 seconds. R.B. loved structurally correct horses. This is a trait that he and Armstrong shared.

While managing Sunny Acres Ranch, Armstrong and Rusty had their own quarter horse breeding program on an adjacent property. Sunny Acres had 500 registered Polled Hereford cows and sold pasture-raised bulls to Florida cattle producers. The untimely death of the ranch owner James M. Wellman due to cancer resulted in the sale of the property. Sunny Acres was located twenty miles from Disney World, which opened that same year, in 1971.

Photo ©KC Montgomery

Charlie Hutton & legendary NRHA Hall of Fame Stallion Nu Chex To Cash

After an unsuccessful stop in Georgia, the Armstrong family moved to Montana with the hope of buying a ranch. He quickly learned that degrees are not nearly as important as money! Next stop was Calhoun, Georgia, as the Northwest Georgia Extension Livestock Specialist with the University of Georgia. This tour included the beginning of telephone auctions for beef cattle with the Red Carpet Cattlemen's Association, Gordon County, Georgia. Son Edward "Ed" Russ was born in Georgia.

Charlie Hutton was the Extension Horse Specialist in Georgia, and Armstrong helped him with his programs. Charlie encouraged Joe to take the position at NMSU. Armstrong considers Hutton to be one of the best breeders of reining horses. Hutton found and introduced Nu Chex To Cash to the reining world.

**COOPERATIVE
EXTENSION
SERVICE**

university of georgia college of agriculture • athens, ga. 30602

March 14, 1979

Dr. Joe Armstrong
Animal Science Department
New Mexico State University
Drawer AE
Las Cruces, NM 88003

Dear Joe:

Letters like this are always tough to write. We have lost several topflight people during my 20 years in Georgia, but I can seriously say that we have never lost one that I hated to see go more than the Armstrongs.

You have been an inspiration to our entire staff and to all the people you worked with. During your tour here I never had the first complaint from an agent or producer. Your accomplishments have been many and the effect will be felt for years to come. One of the greatest things you did was create a peaceful atmosphere in your immediate Gordon County area. I hope that will continue.

We see many articles and much talk now on tele-auctions. I happen to remember that it all started with one Joe Armstrong who couldn't get anyone to talk at the time. I mention this only to say I think you are the most unselfish person I have ever known. The years you were with us you went about getting the job done and were never concerned about who got the credit.

Yes, we are going to miss the Armstrong's very, very much, but we also know that our department is a better one because you came our way. We appreciate the shape you left Northwest Georgia in and hope that you are appreciated in New Mexico as much as you were here.

Sincerely,

O'Dell G. Daniel, Head
Extension Animal Science Department

smg

Wanting to return to the western USA, after receiving a call from Dr. Bobby Rankin, the family moved in 1979 to Las Cruces, New Mexico. He built a very successful horse program at New Mexico State University. Armstrong retired from NMSU in 2001.

SOME OF ARMSTRONG'S MAJOR ACCOMPLISHMENTS AT NMSU:

- Developed one of the most practical University Horse Programs in the USA

- Built a great broodmare band of performance horses through donations, and a good breeding program

- Developed an annual student produced Horse Sale

- Revitalized the New Mexico 4-H Horse Program & started the NM State Fair 4-H Horse Show

- Instituted and coached the NMSU Horse Judging Team

- Started the NM 4-H Horse School – This school was highly successful and was named the "Suzanne Norton Jones 4-H Horsemanship School" in response to Mrs. R.C. Jones' dedication to riders and proper horsemanship. This school was a replica of Charlie Hutton's Georgia 4-H Horse School

- Help start the German Quarter Horse Association's (DQHA) Western Horsemanship Camps, which were patterned after the NM 4-H School

- Created a week-long Wilderness Horse Packing & Outfitting class

- Introduced NMSU to the Intercollegiate Horse Show Association. NMSU won National Championships and had several individual students win National Championships

- Sponsored and recruited for the NMSU Rodeo Team

- Inducted into the New Mexico 4-H Hall of Fame

- New Mexico FFA Honorary State Farmer

- Honored as an Outstanding Professor in the College of Agriculture

Dona Ana County 4-H Club member Criss Armstrong-Grubbs featured on the cover of a NMSU Cooperative Extension Service Brochure – 1984

Photo ©Jim Polito

NMSU Rodeo Team member Ed Armstrong steer wrestling with Jake Aragon hazing, Trey Miller pushing in the chute & Coach Joe, back left, in Las Cruces, NM – 1998

*Newlyweds Rusty & Joe in the Rockies
near Ft. Collins, Colorado – 1964*

*Rusty & Josh at Sunny Acres Ranch
Polk City, Florida – 1970*

*Joe & Criss at Sunny Acres Ranch
Polk City, Florida – 1971*

*Joe & Ed at the NMSU Horse Farm
Mesilla Park, New Mexico – 1980*

OTHER SIGNIFICANT LIFE EVENTS

- ❷ Likely the youngest person to be given an AQHA Judge's card at age 21

- ❷ Joe judged and/or taught horse programs in the U.S.A., Canada, Mexico, El Salvador, Venezuela, Brazil, Uruguay, Argentina, Dominican Republic, Cuba, Russia, Ukraine, Sweden, Denmark, Germany, Luxemburg & Japan

- ❷ Inducted into the German Quarter Horse Association Hall of Fame in 2016

Cutting pioneer & brother-in-law Elbert Sides

Outdoorsman & Lawman Herb Greathouse

Grad school friend & colleague Bobby Rankin on a packtrip in the Gila Wilderness, NM

Photo courtesy of © AQHA

Jackie Kyle Krshka aboard AQHA SUPERHORSE SWEET AND INNOCENT with Tom Krshka, Bill, Jack Kyle, Walt Garrison & AQHA President Bob & Mary Lou Norris – 1982

The NM 4-H Horse School was patterned after Charlie Hutton's very successful Georgia 4-H Horse School. Herb Greathouse, Jack Kyle and Bob Curtiss were instrumental in helping start this school.

Herb Greathouse had quite a history! Born in a tent in the Doctor's backyard in Cuba, NM, he helped his father build a two-story log home when he was six years old (rode the mule to skid the logs in place). Herb was an FBI Agent and loved helping young people. He was an excellent horseman and one of Joe's horse packing mentors and a close friend.

In 1979, at a 4-H horse judging clinic in Albuquerque, AQHA Hall of Famer Jack Kyle brought several horses to be used in the clinic. Jack loved helping kids. He pulled out a two-year-old palomino mare to be used for a "Form to Function" demonstration. With Jack holding the mare, Armstrong proceeded

Photo ©Fulton Robinson

Team Roping Partners Bob Curtiss heeling for Jack Kyle – Photo courtesy of the Curtiss Family

to discuss all the conformation points previously described in this book. Jack and Joe became instant friends from that moment on. Jack would later say, "That was the best conformation talk I ever heard".

The two-year-old Palomino mare turned out to be SWEET AND INNOCENT, who later became the 1982 AQHA SUPERHORSE! Jack Kyle was a true horseman and trainer, and he was a great friend to Armstrong.

Bob Curtiss was a protege of Jack Kyle. They were noted for wearing their jeans tucked into tall red top boots and black hats before these items became commonplace. In addition to being a fine horseman, Bob loved to do cowboy Church Services at horse shows and was an outstanding spur and bit maker – perfectly balanced! As a youngster, Bob's mother helped him learn western pleasure and leads in Michigan from 4-H literature.

Photo ©Debbie Jones

AQHA Hall of Fame couple Suzanne & R.C. "Punch" Jones at their
Horned J Ranch in Tatum, NM – Photo courtesy of Debbie Jones

Punch and Suzanne Jones were the epitome of ranchers and horse people. The Jones' family developed the Debouillet breed of sheep and produced some of the finest wool in the U.S. They also ran cattle and race horses. Mr. and Mrs. R.C. Jones are both in the AQHA Hall of Fame, the NM Racing Hall of Fame, and have many other state and national awards. Their foundation broodmare, MAROON, a track record-setting racehorse who became one of the great broodmares in Southwest history, is also in the AQHA Hall of Fame.

Suzanne was raised in a cavalry family and had the lightest hands with a horse. She lived horses and horsemanship. She and two of her children, Debbie and Clabe, and her dear friend, Anna Eader, became a part of the NM 4-H Horse School and the German Quarter Horse Association's DQHA Horsemanship Camps. Suzanne was inducted into every Hall of Fame for Trainers and Horsewomen.

When they first met, Punch told Joe he would help the NMSU Horse Program any way he could. He was true to his word.

Outstanding Stallion CJ Sugar, sired by Son O Sugar and out of Christy Jay by Rey Jay, at the King Ranch, Kingsville, Texas

The acceptance of CJ Sugar into the NMSU Horse Program was huge! CJ Sugar was a blood brother to Colonel Freckles. Both stallions had Christy Jay as their mother. Colonel Freckles was sired by Jewels Leo Bars (aka "Freckles"), and CJ Sugar was sired by Son O Sugar. Jewels Leo Bars and Son O Sugar were full brothers.

CJ Sugar was an excellent sire and the catalyst for King Ranch's horse manager Joe Stiles and all-time great cutting horse trainer and rider Buster Welch becoming involved with the NMSU Horse Program.

Dr. M.E. Ensminger, Ramon Castro (Fidel Castro's older brother), Rusty & Joe
during an International Ag-Tech School in Havana, Cuba – 1995

In 1993, Dr. M.E. Ensminger, founder of the International Ag-Tech Schools and Agriservices Foundation in Clovis, California, invited Armstrong to be one of his equine instructors on a three week agricultural teaching trip to Russia.

Then, in 1995, he invited Joe and Rusty to be part of the team that made a similar three week tour to Cuba. These two trips were probably more educational for the U.S. instructors than for the Russian and Cuban students. It truly made Armstrong appreciate living in a Judeo-Christian based capitalist country.

While in Cuba, the group was treated to a dinner and rodeo at the King Ranch. Interestingly, the dining room had been untouched by the Castro regime, with the table still set with the original King Ranch place settings. A coffee table with an inlaid pattern of the U.S.A. Flag with 48 stars remained in the dining room.

210

DQHA Horsemanship Camp Instructors Joe, Holger Meyer, Lisa Middelberg, Stacy & Jesse Westfall & Katrin Dreyer-Süchting in Schwerin, Germany – 2015

Armstrong was a part of starting the German Quarter Horse Association's (DQHA) Western Horsemanship Camps in 1999, which are patterned after the New Mexico 4-H Schools. Mrs. Jones had recommended Armstrong's son, Josh Armstrong, to a leading breeder in Germany, Katrin Dreyer-Süchting, because of his horsemanship skills and good hands. Josh spent several weeks in Germany and won both the Working Cow Horse and Reining at the 1994 European Championships. These relationships resulted in the formation of the DQHA Horsemanship Camps, which were the forerunners of the AQHA International Horsemanship Schools.

Katrin Dreyer-Süchting, an excellent breeder and rider, was the Matriarch of the DQHA schools. The AQHA International Schools were the idea of Suzanne Jones and Ulli Vey, the German AQHA Director. German breeder Volker Laves and his family, who own the Circle L Ranch in Wenden, Germany, were helpful in starting the schools.

Kay Wienrich was perhaps Germany's "first reiner". He bought into the program early and was a great advocate. Kay had visited Punch and Suzanne Jones' Horned J Ranch in Tatum, NM, as he was first beginning to switch from English to Western riding.

Armstrong was inducted into the DQHA Hall of Fame in 2016 in appreciation of his leading the camps for 21 years. Gut Borken, managed by Joe's dear friends Christoph and Petra Kühnlein, was a focal point for many of the camps.

Katrin Dreyer-Süchting – one of Germany's earliest Quarter Horse breeders

*Thomas Helmle taking Joe & Megan Duff-Schuller for a ride with his
Haflinger pony after a DQHA Horsemanship Camp in Gut Borken, German*

Kay Wienrich – German Reining Pioneer and NRHA Hall of Fame Member

DQHA Horseman Volker Laves & family at their Circle L Ranch in Wenden, Germany

Front row, left to right: Doug Householder, Pete Gibbs, B.F. Yeates, Gary Potter
Back row: Chelsie Huseman, Dennis Sigler, Jennifer Zoller

Many other people were influential in Armstrong's exploits. The following Educators, who were also horsemen, helped build the educational foundation of the present American western horse industry:

Bobby Rankin and B.F. Yeates (Texas A&M) were two of the early educators who wrote much of the initial 4-H Horse literature and conducted hundreds of horse clinics for youth and adults. Bobby and B.F. were both National Intercollegiate Rodeo Association contestants and were nationally successful. B.F. competed in the first NIRA National Championship as a Texas Tech contestant! They plowed much of the early ground in straight furrows.

Jim Heird (Texas Tech, Colorado State, and Texas A&M) was a forerunner and was the mainstay in setting up the AJQHA and Collegiate Horse Judging Contests.

Other role models as good on a horse as they were in the classroom include Dave Whitaker (Middle Tennessee State University), Doug Householder and Dennis Sigler (Texas A&M). Charlie Hutton (University of Georgia) was an excellent writer, communicator, showman and geneticist. There are others just as qualified, but these were special to Armstrong.

214

Dave Whitaker – Middle Tennessee State

Doug Householder – Texas A&M

Charlie Hutton – University of Georgia

Jim Heird – Texas Tech/CSU/Texas A&M

Larry Rose riding AQHA Champion & NRHA Legend & Leading Sire GREAT PINE

Larry Rose of Lexington, Ohio, is a very intelligent (maybe a genius) breeder and trainer, as well as a good friend. He is a geneticist like Hutton. At one time, more Non-Pro riders were winning on Larry Rose-bred horses than any other. Larry is synonymous with GREAT PINE as Hutton is with NU CHEX TO CASH. Larry spent three winters at Armstrong Equine Service (waiting for Ohio to thaw out) training his futurity horses. GREAT RED PINE was one of them.

Lew Sterrett & DESIRED SPARK, Anadarko, OK

Armstrong holds Lew Sterrett of Anadarko, Oklahoma, in high esteem. Lew is an excellent horseman and showed Appaloosas early in his career after graduating from Pennsylvania State University. Lew's ministry today is appropriately named **Sermon on the Mount**. He has carried the Gospel of Jesus Christ to the world with his "life lessons in horse language". Lew walks his talk, using scripture daily. Like all strong teachers and competitors, Lew constantly works on his horsemanship skills. Doug Millholland has been a mentor to Lew.

» *www.sermononthemount.org*

Two horsemen Armstrong had the pleasure of serving on their Graduate Committees who have made great impacts are Craig Wood (University of Kentucky) and Jason Bruemmer (Colorado State University).

Wood supervised the Kentucky 4-H Horse Program and is the current assistant director of UK Agriculture and Natural Resources Extension. He is an originator in "distance education" and a past President of the American Paint Horse Association.

Craig Wood with his mare DEE in Owenton, Kentucky

Bruemmer is highly successful as a Reproductive Specialist, internationally recognized for his research and innovations in the field. He is one of a few who are great teachers and researchers but are also able to relate to the horsemen, veterinarians and students alike. A former professor and Associate Director of Equine Sciences at CSU, he is now the project leader in fertility control with the USDA-APHIS National Wildlife Research Center.

Jason Bruemmer preparing an immunocastration dart to manage feral hippo populations in Puerto Triunfo, Colombia

The combination of education and horsemanship produces amazing results. It is the meeting of preparation and opportunity!

BILL BREWER
EXECUTIVE VICE PRESIDENT

January 30, 2008

Joe:

I received your letter of resignation as an AQHA approved judge. I would like to take this opportunity to personally thank you for your 40 years of service as one of our approved judges.

Your continued support of the American Quarter Horse Association, the American Quarter Horse industry and our personal friendship is greatly appreciated.

I will never forget our ride in the Gila Wilderness as it is one of my stories that I don't have to embellish. If you are ever in Amarillo, please take time to stop by.

Best wishes to you and your family for a most enjoyable and successful 2008.

All the best.

Bill

Bill

c: Alex Ross

P.O. BOX 200 · AMARILLO, TX 79168

In 1994, Armstrong had the pleasure of hosting the AQHA Executive Committee for a week of horse packing and camping in the Gila Wilderness where they experienced true "trail" riding!

Armstrong was acquainted with Bill Brewer long before Bill headed AQHA. Brewer was an American Polled Hereford Association Field Man when Armstrong was breeding Polled Herefords as the Sunny Acres Ranch Manager in Polk City, FL

NMSU Horse Packing & Outfitting Class heading into the Gila Wilderness for 7 days – 1983

Joe & NMSU DIRK a little off the trail in the Gila, New Mexico – 1984

Ed & MR ROYAL BUG leading a packstring through McKenna Park in the Gila, NM – 1985

After retirement as an AQHA judge, Joe now enjoys showing his horses.
He is qualified & planning to compete in the 2023 AQHA World Show

Ed roping on 22 year old MR ROYAL BUG, the Armstrong family's first show horse. BUG was shown by all the children in English & Western classes at 4-H & AQHA shows before retiring as a rodeo heel horse. He lived to be 36 and is buried at the family farm

J.H.B. "Joe 3" Armstrong, III

Edward "Eddie" Jeronimo Armstrong

Photo courtesy of ©Kristin Dickerson/Spirit & Nature Productions

222

Photo courtesy of ©Kristin Dickerson/Spirit & Nature Productions

Georgia Criss Armstrong

Photo courtesy of ©Kristin Dickerson/Spirit & Nature Productions

Peter Russ Armstrong

Photos © Jeff Kirkbride Photography

Josh & RX SUGAR Freestyle Reining Bridleless at the All American Quarter Horse Congress to Johnny Cash's "Folsom Prison Blues" in Columbus, Ohio – 2003

Josh & MR SUNOLENA LETTERS Freestyle Reining Bridleless at the World Equestrian Games to Willie Nelson's "Pancho & Lefty" in Lexington, Kentucky – 2010

Armstrong's two sons also affected his career. Both sons grew up with the influence of the 4-H Horse School and the influence of the men and women who were instructors. They had many mentors.

Josh, the older, decided early to make horses his life's work. He was a 4-H National Horse Record Book winner, won the Reining and Working Cow Horse classes at the European Championship in 1994, and was the first person to ever go completely bridleless (no string attached) in a major Freestyle Reining event. He won the All American Quarter Horse Congress twice on SUERTE FUERTE, a stallion he raised and trained. He also made the 45th AQHA SUPREME CHAMPION – GOTUM GONE – in 1995.

Josh continues to train, breed, show and ranch, with his children following in his footsteps. Josh and his wife Linda are the parents of Rusty and Joe's four grandchildren: Joe III, Georgia Criss, Edward Jeronimo and Peter Russ.

Joe & Ed flying a paraglider over Aspen, Colorado, to celebrate Joe's 75th birthday – 2012

Joe's younger son, Ed, has the same talent but pursues other exciting sports. Ed was a good roper, winning the average in team roping for NMSU at the 1998 NIRA Grand Canyon Regional Finals rodeo, and was his Dad's right hand man on the NMSU Wilderness horse pack trips. But he excelled on the snow! An avid skier and whitewater enthusiast, his love of mountains led him to pioneer the sport of speed flying in the U.S. – simultaneously skiing and flying off the peaks throughout the Rocky Mountains. He continues to enjoy flying and holds a cross-country distance record in the sport of paragliding.

Josh & AQHA SUPREME CHAMPION GOTUM GONE heading for Ed & CADA VEZ with Israeli horse breeder, Nadi Bar, working the chute

Criss Lynn at a 4-H Horse Show – 1984

Joe's daughter, Criss Lynn Grubbs, followed her Dad into education and was an excellent school teacher and administrator. She was active with horses as a youth in 4-H, assisting at horse schools, horse shows and on pack trips. Like her Dad, she had a talent for basketball, playing college ball on an athletic scholarship. She received a Master's degree in Education and is retired from the Las Cruces Public School system. She and her husband, Monty, live in Lubbock, TX, where she is a Field Account Executive for Renaissance Learning.

Rusty Vieh in Hollandale, Mississippi –1961

Rusty is Joe's wife and his pride and joy. They grew up 100 miles apart in Mississippi but did not meet until they were students in Fort Collins at Colorado State University. Rusty was nearing completion of her B.S. in Animal Science when Joe moved there to pursue his Ph.D. in Animal Breeding. Some friends told Joe's mother about Rusty, and she relayed the message to Joe. The rest is good history. Rusty is a National Marketing Director with The Juice Plus+ Company.

Photo Courtesy of © Julie Baish

Joe & Rusty at their home in La Mesa, New Mexico, nearing their 60th year of marriage and 60th year of raising horses together

Rusty qualified for the AQHA World Show in Sorting and has competed in cutting, team penning, barrels, goat tying, endurance riding and driving.

Rusty is also the one who told Joe how he could have a personal relationship with Jesus Christ. It took a while, but with Rusty, her friends, and Campus Crusade for Christ, Joe invited Jesus Christ into his life to be his Savior and Lord in 1961.

He will tell you that knowing Jesus and marrying Rusty are the two best things that ever happened to him. Everything else is the goodness that came from those two decisions.

At 86, Joe enjoys competing on RANKINS REMINIC in Ranch Riding and Working Cow Horse, pack trips into the Wilderness with his grandchildren, raising performance horses, and hosting family, friends and horse activities at his farm in New Mexico. Let him know what you think of his first book:

jba@armstrongequine.com

Joe & Rusty giving BABE & SANSY a drink from Minnehaha Gulch in the Elk Mountains in the Maroon Bells-Snowmass Wilderness, White River Nat'l Forest, Colorado — Elevation 11,111 FT

AQHA Hall of Fame Member "Sunny" Jim Orr, 6 years old driving a hay stacker team at the Longmore Ranch in Longmore, Colorado, 1940 – Photo courtesy of Rayann Orr

Photo © Rayann Orr

WEIGHTS & MEASURES

Length
1 Inch (in)	= 0.08333 ft	= 2.54 Centimeters (cm)
1 Hand	= 4 in	= 10.16 cm
1 Foot (ft)	= 12 in	= 0.3048 Meters (m)
1 Yard (yd)	= 3 ft = 36 in	= 0.9144 m
1 Furlong (fur)	= 220 yd = ⅛ mi	= 201.168 m or 0.201168 km
1 Mile (mi)	= 5,280 ft = 1,760 yd	= 1.6093 Kilometers (km)

Area
1 Square Inch (in²⁾	= 0.006944 ft²	= 6.4516 cm²
1 Square Foot (ft²)	= 144 in²	= 0.0929 m²
1 Acre	= 43,560 ft²	= 0.405 Hectares (ha)
1 Square Mile (mi²)	= 1 Section = 640 Acres	= 2.58999 km² or 259.2 ha

Volume
1 Cubic Inch (in³)	= 0.0005787 ft³ = 0.554 fl oz	= 16.3871 cm³ or mL
1 Cubic Foot (ft³)	= 1,728 in³ or 7.481 gal	= 0.0283168 m³ = 28.3168 L
1 Cubic Yard (yd³)	= 27 ft³ or 201.974 gal	= 0.764555 m³ = 764.555 L
1 Acre-Inch	= 27,154 gal or 3630 ft³	= 1,027.9 Hectoliters (hL)
1 Acre-Foot	= 325,851 gal or 43,560 ft³	= 12,334.8 hL or 1,233.48 m³

Liquid
1 CC (cubic centimeter)	= 0.202884 tsp	= 1 mL
1 Teaspoon (tsp)	= 0.333 tbsp	= 4.92892 mL
1 Tablespoon (tbsp)	= 3 tsp = 0.5 fl oz	= 14.7868 mL
1 Fluid Ounce (fl oz)	= 2 tbsp	= 29.5735 mL
1 Cup (cp)	= 8 fl oz	= 236.5882 mL
1 Pint (pt)	= 2 cp = 16 fl oz	= 473.1765 mL
1 Quart (qt)	= 2 pt = 4cp = 32 fl oz	= 0.9464 L
1 Gallon (gal)	= 4 qt = 128 fl oz = 231 in³	= 3.7854 L

Weight/Mass
1 Grain	= 0.002286 oz	= 64.7989 Milligrams (mg)
1 Ounce (oz)	= 0.0625 lbs	= 28.3495 Grams (g0
1 Pound (lb)	= 16 Ounces	= 0.453592 Kilograms (kg)
1 Hundredweight (cwt)	= 100 lbs	= 45.36 kg
1 U.S. Ton (tn)	= 2,000 lbs	= 0.907185 Metric Tons (mt)
1 Metric Ton (mt)	= 2,204.62 lbs = 1.1 tn	= 1,000 kg

Hay – Small Square Bale
1 Two-Wire Bale	= Average 67 lbs, ±10% (30 Bales per Ton)
1 Three-Wire Bale	= Average 110 lbs, ±10% (18.2 Bales per Ton)

Temperature

Fahrenheit = (°Celsius x 1.8) + 32   Celsius = (°Fahrenheit − 32) x 0.555

Mosaic of NRHA Champion VON REMINIC & Todd Sommers composed from photos of some of the many people helped by & horses raised by the author

INDEX

Additional information and resources for horse owners are available at:
https://horsemanshandbook.com

Josh Armstrong & VON GUS demonstrating the versatility of the American Quarter Horse during AQHA Day 2020 at Ruidoso Downs Racetrack – Photo courtesy of Jake Rogers

What Professionals, Peers & Former Students say about the author and the Horseman's Handbook:

"For decades, Dr. Armstrong has been a leader in advancing the American Quarter Horse around the world."
— **Clay Mathis**, Director at King Ranch Institute for Ranch Management, Kingsville, TX

"A book that shares the true necessities and requirements of horse ownership...an excellent guide to manage expectations."
— **Morgan Pennington**, Equine Instructor & Coach, Laramie County Community College, Cheyenne, WY

"Joe has been a friend and mentor to me and my wife in the equestrian world. His knowledge and expertise is without equal."
— **Dr. William T. Baker**, MD, Las Cruces, NM

"All my knowledge came from Joe. He has been a real assistance in improving Quarter Horses in our region of Israel."
— **Nadi Bar**, Horseman, Golan Heights, Israel

"I was in enlightened by Joe's approach...this book will be my 'first aid kit'."
— **David Avery**, Former Judge & Director of International Affairs at AQHA, DQHA Hall of Fame Honoree, Amarillo, TX

"He has had a very profound effect on the regional and international equine world."
— **Dr. James Prichard**, DVM, Las Cruces, NM

"Joe Armstrong is a great horseman and brings decades of knowledge to this book. I'll go to it often."
— **Jesse Westfall**, NRHA Judge & Trainer in Residence at Asbury University, Perrysville, OH

"Joe...has given time, expertise and heart to build a strong equine community in New Mexico and beyond."
— **Western Horseman Magazine – Kate Bradley Byars**, Writer & Photographer, Fredericksburg, TX

"A person of bold, impeccable character. Has positively impacted thousands nationally and internationally, me included."
— **Dr. Doug Householder** (deceased), Texas A&M Professor Emeritus, Extension Horse Specialist

"NMSU professor Joe Armstrong built one of the finest academic horse programs in the country."
— **John Owens**, Former Dean of NMSU College of Agriculture, Las Cruces, NM

"A complete and uncomplicated text. I highly recommend this book for any serious horse owner."
— **Dr. Dennis Sigler**, Texas A&M Professor & Horse Extension Specialist, College Station, TX

"Dr. Joe Bates Armstrong is a horseman's horseman, second to none! Great all-around horseman and AQHA judge."
— **Larry Rose**, Reining Horse Breeder (owner of Great Pine), Competitor, Coach & Writer, Mansfield, OH

"A living legend. One of the founders of the DQHA Horsemanship Camps."
— **Deutsche Quarter Horse Association**, Aschaffenburg, Germany

"From one of the most seasoned, trustworthy people in the horse industry. There is a whole lot of wisdom in this book."
— **Dr. Lew Sterrett**, Horseman and Pastor, Sermon on the Mount, Anadarko, OK

"Dr. Armstrong believed in me when no one else did and gave me the courage to step forward in the horse world."
— **Todd Marler**, Reining Horse Trainer and Pastor, El Paso, TX

"It would require a book series to tell the full story of [Joe's] impact on so many people."
— **Mark Rice**, NMSU Horse Judging Team Member, Ft. Collins, CO

"Dr. Armstrong has been a hero of mine...I have tried to be a mentor to students as he was to myself and countless others."
— **Nathan Wells**, Coordinator of Equine Studies, Texas A&M Commerce, TX

"His influence will not only be forever felt in the sandy arenas, but in the hearts and minds of those that shared his journey."
— **Dr. David Whitaker**, Middle Tennessee State University Professor Emeritus

"There is not enough time in the day to list Dr. Armstrong's contribution to the horse industry."
— **Trey Miller**, NMSU Rodeo Club Team Member, Horseman and Banker, San Miguel, NM

Add your review here: *https://horsemanshandbook.com*

240